PHOTOSHOP 5
3D TEXTURES

f/x

and design

GEOFFREY SMITH

The Coriolis Group, Inc.
An International Thomson Publishing Company
14455 N. Hayden Road, Suite 220
Scottsdale, Arizona 85260

602/483-0192
FAX 602/483-0193
http://www.coriolis.com

Library of Congress Cataloging-In-Publication Data
Smith, Geoffrey, 1965-
    Photoshop 5 3D textures f/x and design / by Geoffrey Smith.
        p.   cm.
    Includes index.
    ISBN 1-57610-274-2
    1. Computer graphics.   2. Adobe Photoshop.
3. Three-dimensional display systems.   I. Title.
T385.F5924   1999
006.6'93--dc21   98-26403
                                                        CIP

Printed in the United States of America
10 9 8 7 6 5 4 3 2 1

Publisher
Keith Weiskamp

Acquisitions Editor
Stephanie Wall

Marketing Specialist
Dylan Zoller

Project Editor
Mariann Hansen Barsolo

Technical Reviewer
Cheryl Kirk

Production Coordinator
Jon Gabriel

Cover Design
Anthony Stock
Additional art provided by Brandon Riza

Layout Design
April Nielsen

CD-ROM Developer
Robert Clarfield

an International Thomson Publishing company

Albany, NY • Belmont, CA • Bonn • Boston • Cincinnati • Detroit • Johannesburg
London • Madrid • Melbourne • Mexico City • New York • Paris • Singapore
Tokyo • Toronto • Washington

OTHER TITLES FOR THE CREATIVE PROFESSIONAL

3D Studio MAX R2.5 f/x and design
by Jon A. Bell

Adobe PageMill 3 f/x and design
by Daniel Gray

Character Animation In Depth
by Doug Kelly

Photoshop 5 Filters f/x and design
by T. Michael Clark

Photoshop 5 In Depth
by David Xenakis & Sherry London

QuarkXPress 4 In Depth
by William Harrell & Elaine Betts

PHOTOSHOP 5
3D TEXTURES
F/X AND DESIGN

This book is dedicated to my wife Kimberly. Without her love and support this book could never have been written. I would also like to thank my parents for their continued support.

ॐ

About The Author

Geoffrey Smith is the lead artist and president of PixlSmith Productions, which specializes in the creation of photorealistic surfacing for 3D creatures and objects. He graduated from the State University College at Buffalo, New York, with a bachelor's degree in the fine arts. He worked as graphic design manager for a toy company in Buffalo and later returned to school to study computer graphics and animation at the University of Toronto in Canada. Smith is an expert user of Photoshop, LightWave, Animation Master, and Raydream Studio. He is also a contributing author of *3D Creature Workshop* (Charles River Inc.) and the image mapping specialist for *Serious 3D Magazine* (Serious Publishing Group).

Acknowledgments

I would like to thank Bill Fleming of Komodo Studio not only for providing me with the 3D models of Gorg, Dr. Dread, Scratch, and Pawn, but also for sharing with me his inexhaustible knowledge and skill in the realm of 3D graphics and helping me to share the knowledge of surfacing and 3D with all of you. I would also like to thank the brilliant staff at New Agora Corporation for its advice and continuing assistance.

FOREWORD

Image maps are the crowning element of a 3D model. They can either make or break your surfacing. Nothing is worse than spending days on the perfect model only to have the surfacing undermine its credibility. On the other hand, nothing is quite as rewarding as a surfacing job done well. It will literally bring your model to life—particularly if it's a creature or character.

While there are many possibilities for creating image maps, Photoshop stands out as the undisputed king. It offers everything you need to create absolutely dazzling image maps. The key is to fully understand the principles of image map surfacing so you can ensure your image maps work properly. *Photoshop 5 3D Textures f/x and design* offers you this understanding by demonstrating many never before revealed techniques for creating seamless image maps with Photoshop.

Geoff Smith is one of the most talented surfacing minds in the 3D industry. His insights revealed in *Photoshop 5 3D Textures f/x and design* will open your eyes to a number of new possibilities and take you well beyond your surfacing expectations.

Bill Fleming
President, Komodo Studio
Editor in Chief, Serious 3D Magazine

Contents At A Glance

Photoshop 5
3D Textures
F/X and Design

TABLE OF CONTENTS

Photoshop 5
3D Textures
F/X and Design

Introduction

Creating computer generated imagery is no small task. Contrary to the popular belief of the uninitiated, the computer does not do all of the work for you. In fact, most of the time it seems as if the computer is actually the biggest hurdle standing between you and the masterful image conceived in your mind's eye. Much of the reason that so many of today's 3D graphics look the same or like digital plastic toys is that most 3D artists lack a thorough understanding of image mapping techniques.

Welcome to *Photoshop 5 3D Textures f/x and design.* Unlike other Photoshop books, which are designed to give the reader some basic Photoshop texturing skills for use on the Web and in illustration, this book will provide you with in-depth, photorealistic 3D texturing skills to rival those seen in Hollywood blockbusters.

In the past few years, 3D programs have evolved to include image mapping technology previously found only in the most sophisticated (and expensive) programs. As 3D programs have progressed, so too has Photoshop. Photoshop 5 now offers such a plethora of painting and image manipulation tools that creating photorealistic image maps is quicker and easier than ever. All you need is the knowledge and imagination to put the tools to use.

Contained herein you'll find a surplus of step-by-step image mapping tutorials, dozens of hyper-realistic 3D models, and time tested Photoshop techniques and image mapping tips. By reading this book, you will save yourself countless hours of frustration in trial and error image mapping otherwise spent in trying to get your 3D scenes to look exactly the way you want them to. I've already put in those countless hours for you. The result of years of image manipulation and mapping experience is at your fingertips. Take advantage of it.

Who Should Use This Book?

Whether you are a Photoshop novice or have been working with the program professionally for years, *Photoshop 5 3D Textures f/x and design* will enhance your working knowledge and provide you with the necessary skills to create visually stunning 3D creations. Whether you work as a 3D animator, an illustrator for print or the Web, or simply have a desire to improve the quality of your 3D creations in your spare time, this book is for you. *Photoshop 5 3D Textures f/x and design* has been created as a cross-platform educational tool. So whether you're using Alias/Wavefront, Softimage, 3D Studio MAX, LightWave, Truespace, ElectricImage, Hash Animation Master, Strata Studio, or RayDream, this book has something for you.

How This Book Is Set Up

Photoshop 5 3D Textures f/x and design begins with some quick Photoshop basics. Chapter 1, "Photoshop Painting Basics," gives readers who are somewhat new to Photoshop a good starting point for using layers to create image maps, working with opacity settings, creating custom brushes, exploring variations, using hue and saturation to define image map types, using the brightness and contrast dialog box, adjusting levels, using the Eyedropper tool, and knowing the difference between airbrush and paintbrush effects.

Chapter 2, "Advanced Painting Techniques," moves on to more advanced Photoshop concepts such as using the Smudge tool with options, aging textures with the Burn tool, painting with the Clone tool, and creating complex textures with fractals. In Chapter 3, "Special Editing Techniques," you learn about using scanners and scanned imagery to add the texture qualities of the real world to the surfaces of your own 3D worlds.

Chapter 4, "Image Map Types," provides you with what your 3D application's manual forgot to mention about the different types of image mapping and how they really work. In this chapter, you learn the true nature of Color, Bump, Specularity, Diffusion, Displacement, Transparency, Clip, and Luminosity maps.

In Chapter 5, "Working With Image Maps," you acquire the skills needed to place your 2D image maps onto the surfaces of your 3D creations. This chapter covers planar, cylindrical, sphere, and cubic mapping techniques, and also gives you a variety of time tested procedures on how to avoid image map stretching. You also learn how to create seamless image mapped surfaces that will leave even the most experienced 3D artists wondering how you pulled it off. Chapter 6, "Using Layered Images Maps," introduces you to the unsurpassed realism obtainable with the use of layered image maps.

In Chapter 7, "Painting Industrial Textures," you get your hands dirty by learning to create industrial textures and adding dirt, grime, and the ravages of time to your 3D surfaces. Chapter 8, "Painting Science Fiction Textures," provides you with necessary skills to create astounding surfaces for your science fiction scenes. You learn how to create blast marks, metal plating, and exhaust burn marks for spaceships; a variety of planet surfaces for your spaceships to encounter; and sparkling nebula and star fields.

In Chapter 9, "Painting Organic Creature Textures," you discover what it takes to create truly awesome organic textures. This chapter is the definitive guide on how to define your 3D characters' and creatures' biography and background. You learn how and where to find reference material; how to create 3D skin that looks as if you could touch it; and how to create wrinkles, pores, scars, sweat, muscles, veins, eyes, scales, and just about any attribute of organic flesh.

Chapter 10, "Painting Character Accessories," goes further in the discussion of creating utterly believable 3D characters and creatures when you learn to create image maps for characters' clothing complete with wrinkles, a variety of stains, color, and cloth patterns. And if you've ever struggled with creating realistic natural textures such as rock, sand, dirt and foliage, you need look no further than Chapter 11, "Painting Natural Textures," to end the struggle.

Chapter 12, "Painting Displacement Map Textures," gives you a thorough understanding of Displacement maps by showing you how to use them to create complex geometry that would otherwise be too difficult or time consuming to produce in any other way.

In the final chapter, Chapter 13, "Painting Light Gels," you learn how to create image maps for the use of light gels. Light gels are a great way to enhance the richness and depth of your 3D scenes. This chapter will teach you how to create shadow maps and color gels in conjunction with animated and still imagery.

Photoshop 5 3D Textures f/x and design also contains a Color Studio in which I have extracted final renders and important color maps, layers, and textures to enhance your knowledge and give you a better visual representation of the concepts covered.

Photoshop 5 3D Textures f/x and design comes complete with a PC- and Macintosh-friendly CD-ROM containing dozens of royalty-free, seamlessly tileable texture maps, and some of the most stunning 3D models you've ever seen. These models have been provided in a variety of formats, including LightWave, Alias/Wavefront, 3D Studio MAX, DXF, and 3DMF. Along with the textures, animations have been provided of scenes mentioned in the text that contain animated texture maps. You'll also find demos of Adobe's Photoshop 5.

Photoshop 5
3D Textures
F/X and Design

PART I

Photoshop
3D Texture
Painting
Techniques

PHOTOSHOP
PAINTING BASICS

1

Way back when, when computers were known mainly as business machines and artists could be recognized by their paint-covered smocks, no one would have thought that future artists who made their living from their art would spend most of their time manipulating pixels with digital brushes. Today, digital artists make up the vast majority of working artists, and Adobe Photoshop is one of the tools that has shaped the way they work.

Graphics programs were pretty limited when they first came out—unless you were into big, clunky pixels and were happy to be limited to two values of color: black and white. Then, graphics programs took a giant leap forward with the introduction of Adobe Photoshop for the Apple Macintosh.

Even in its infancy, Photoshop was impressive. Today, its features have grown to make it arguably the best image-editing, -creating, and manipulating program available. For most of the tutorials in this book, you can use Photoshop 5 and 4. If, however, you've never upgraded from version 3, you still can successfully complete 99.9 percent of the tutorials in this book. In this chapter, you examine some of Photoshop's more basic features:

- Layers
- Opacity
- Brushes
- Variations
- Hue/Saturation
- Brightness/Contrast
- Levels
- Eyedropper tool
- Airbrush and Paintbrush Effects

Using Layers

When Adobe introduced the layers feature with Photoshop 3, it set yet another standard for painting programs. To top it off, Adobe also, perhaps unknowingly, made creating and manipulating image maps a hundred times easier for 3D artists. With layers, you can ensure that the image maps you create will line up exactly with one another. By using layers, you can lay one image on top of another and perform individual changes to each layer without changing the layers above or beneath it. So what's the value of this capability? Well, in this chapter, you take a look.

In this section, you learn about layers the best way I know how to teach you: by manipulating them.

1. Open the file called Face.psd, which you can find in chapt1\Layers on the companion CD.

2. Open the Layers palette by selecting Window|Show Layers or by pressing the F7 key on your keyboard. Notice the three layers for this file:

- *Wireframe* contains a screen capture of the wireframe for the face model.

- *Template* is the layer above Wireframe. It shows a rendered image of the model of the face.

- *Color* is the layer above Template. It is the color image map you can manipulate and then map onto the 3D model.

3. Make the Color layer active by clicking on it. The Color layer then covers up the two layers that are beneath it. You can manipulate only the data that's in the Color layer. Your desktop should resemble Figure 1.1 at this point.

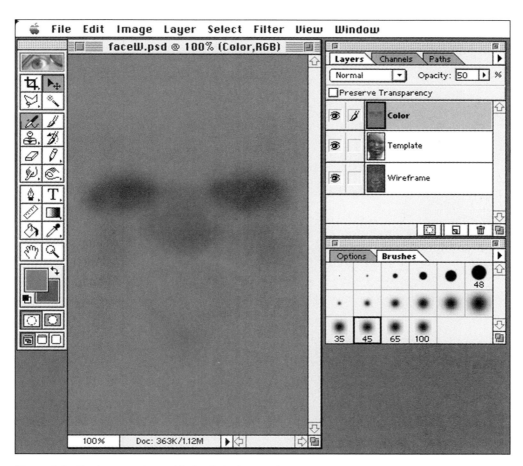

Figure 1.1   The Layers palette with the Color layer active.

What if you decide that the lip color for the Color layer is a little too light for your purposes, and you want to darken the lips a bit? How can you be sure that where you darken the lips' color the color map will line up exactly with the 3D model? After all, you don't want the 3D character to look as though he is wearing poorly applied lipstick. You have the Template and Wireframe layers for that reason; they tell you exactly where the Color image will line up with the 3D image after the maps are applied to the model. So how can you see the Template and Wireframe layers for reference while you're working with the Color? By using the Opacity slider from within the Layers palette, as shown in Figure 1.2.

Working With Opacity

By using the Opacity pop-up slider, you can make the active layer semi-transparent, thus allowing you to see the layer that lies directly beneath the active layer. Right now, the Template layer appears beneath the Color layer. If you set the Color layer's Opacity to 50%, you can see the Template layer through the semitransparent Color layer. But what if you want to view the Wireframe layer through the Color layer? One approach is to click on the little eye symbol on the far left of the Template layer, making the Template layer invisible (as shown in Figure 1.3).

Alternatively, you could drag the Wireframe layer from the bottom of the Layers palette until it sits directly beneath the Color layer, as shown in Figure 1.4.

Sometimes, the bottommost layer (where the Wireframe layer was) doesn't budge because it is a Background layer by default. The Background layer cannot be moved. To free its movement, follow these steps:

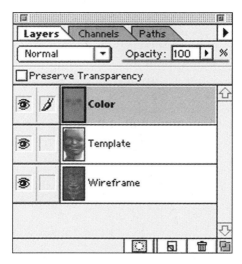

Figure 1.2 The Opacity slider in the Layers palette.

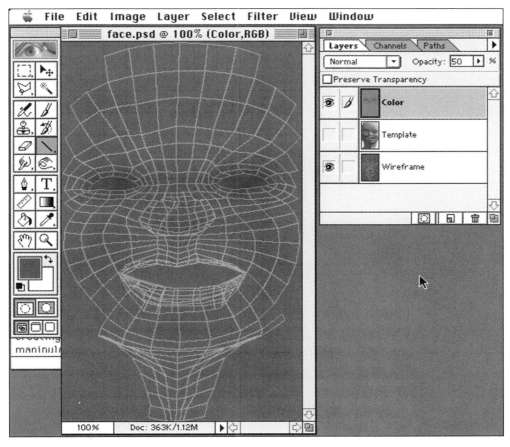

Figure 1.3 Clicking on the eye symbol to the left of the Template layer makes the layer invisible, as shown here.

1. Make the Background layer active by clicking on it.

2. Select Layer|Duplicate Layer. You now should have a copy of the Background layer, which you can move around freely.

3. To remove the original Background layer, make it active and then select Layer|Delete Layer.

To change the color of the character's lips, move the Wireframe layer back to its original position by dragging it to the bottom of the layers. Set the Color layer's Opacity to 100% if it is not already. Do so by making the Color layer active and sliding the Opacity slider all the way up to 100%. Now, if you want to darken the character's lips, follow these few steps:

1. Double-click on the Burn tool icon in the toolbox (the one that looks like a hand pinching something). This action opens the Burn Options palette, as shown in Figure 1.5.

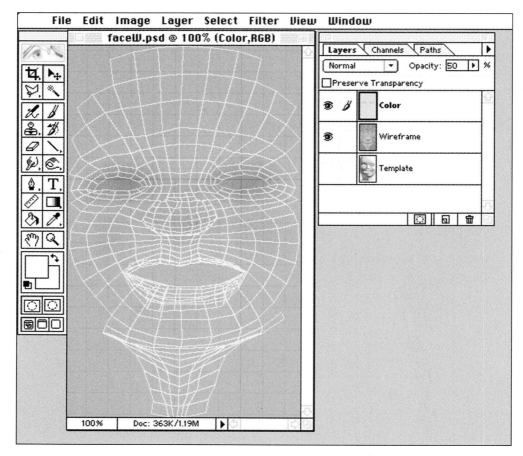

Figure 1.4 The Wireframe layer after moving it beneath the Color layer (see figure in Color Studio).

2. Select Midtones with an Exposure setting of 18%.

3. Click on the Brushes tab at the top of the dialog box. You then can choose from a variety of brushes. You can simply click on the brush that you want to use, or you can make your own brush by double-clicking on any of the brushes in the Brushes palette.

Creating Brushes

To create your own unique brush, follow these steps:

1. Double-click on the Paintbrush tool to open the Paintbrush Options palette, as shown in Figure 1.6.

2. Select Window|Show Brushes|New Brush and give the brush the following settings:

   - Diameter: 13 pixels

   - Hardness: 0%

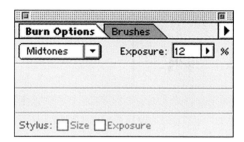

Figure 1.5 The Burn Options palette for the Burn tool.

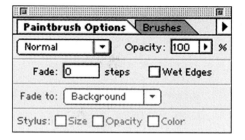

Figure 1.6 The Paintbrush Options palette.

- Spacing: 25%

- Default Angle and Roundness

3. To test the new brush settings, use the brush to make a mark on the Color layer. Be careful to create no more than one continuous brush stroke because you'll undo the results of this stroke later. If you were to create another stroke or even click the mouse once after this initial stroke, you could not undo the stroke later. If you like the results of this test stroke, keep the Burn tool settings. If not, you can change the brush's Diameter or Pressure settings.

4. Make the Color layer semitransparent by setting its Opacity to 50%. You should be able to see the Template layer through the semitransparent Color layer at this point.

5. Using the Burn tool, darken the area of the character's lips. Because the lip area is pretty small for this character, you need to see exactly where you are applying the Burn tool changes on the lips. To help you see just how much of the lips your brush will cover, change the preferences for the look of the brush by selecting File|Preferences|Display & Cursors. The dialog box shown in Figure 1.7 then appears.

6. Under Painting Cursors, click on Brush Size. Now you can see the area that the brush will cover before you begin making brush strokes.

7. After you darken the entire lip area with the Burn brush you created, set the Opacity of the Color layer back to 100% to see whether you're happy with the change or whether you've missed any areas. If any areas were missed, set the Opacity of the layer to about 90%, and touch up any trouble spots. Set the Color layer's Opacity back to 100%, and see whether the lips look all right now.

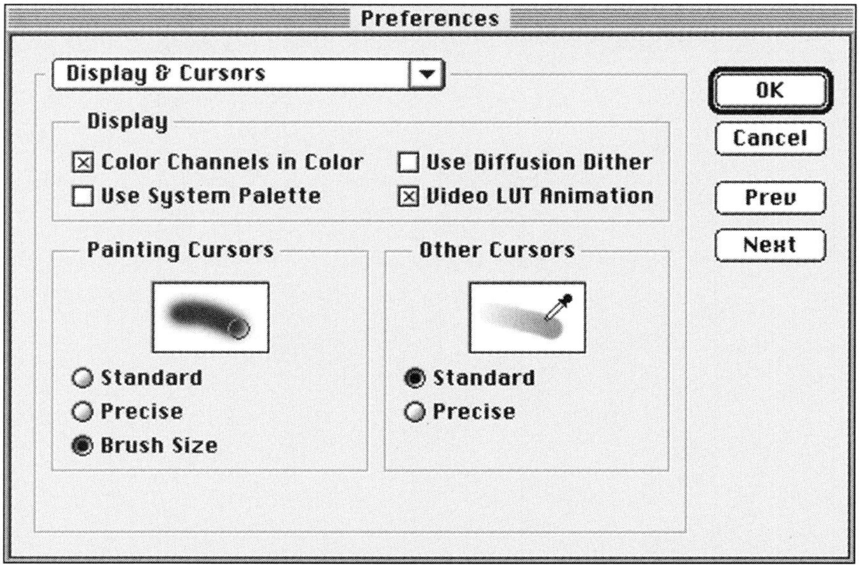

Figure 1.7   Preferences for Display & Cursors.

Suppose that you have a sudden flash of insight at this point telling you that the character's face is way too yellow. He looks jaundiced, for Pete's sake! Photoshop gives you at least half a dozen ways to deal with color problems. One of those ways is with Variations.

Exploring Variations

To open the Variations dialog box, select Image|Adjust|Variations (see Figure 1.8).

Variations are set up as a series of 12 boxes, each containing a slightly different colored icon of the active layer. The two at the top are the Original image and the Current Pick. The boxes on the far right control the amount of black and white that you can apply to the image. The rest of the boxes are for controlling the image's color. If you want to add more red to the image, simply click once on the More Red box. The Current Pick box, at the top of the dialog box, immediately updates to show the result. If you're unsatisfied with the changes, click on the Original image box to get back to where you started.

Using Variations, you also can switch among several modes: Shadows applies changes with an emphasis on the darker parts of the image, Midtones applies changes to the middle tones, and Highlights allows you to work with color in regard to the lighter areas of the image. The Saturation mode allows you to make the hues richer (like adding more pigment to your paint). The slider marked from Fine to Coarse allows you to

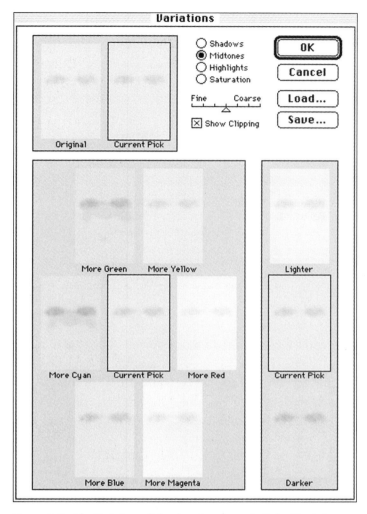

Figure 1.8   The Variations dialog box (see figure in Color Studio).

control how drastic your changes will be. For example, if you were to click on Add Red with the slider set all the way to Coarse, the change would be extreme. If you set it to Fine, the change would be nearly imperceptible.

Variations can be a lot of fun to play with, but I usually end up spending too much time in the Variations dialog box. If you know precisely what color changes you want to make, the Hue/Saturation dialog box, though more primitive, will usually get you there quicker.

Setting Hue/Saturation

The Hue/Saturation dialog box is much smaller and simpler than the Variations dialog box, as you can see in Figure 1.9, but it can give you essentially the same amount of control over the layer that you're working on.

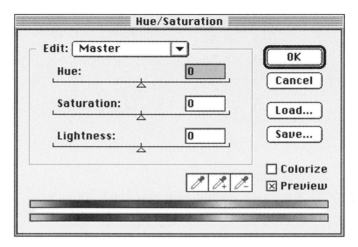

Figure 1.9 The Hue/Saturation dialog box.

To open the Hue/Saturation dialog box, select Image|Adjust|Hue/Saturation. You then see three rows of sliders: Hue, Saturation, and Lightness. The Hue slider controls the color spectrum of the image (sort of like controlling the color's point on the color wheel). With this slider, you can change the face's color from peach to vermilion if you want. Next is the Saturation slider, which controls the richness of the color. If you slide the Saturation slider all the way to the left, you remove all the color from the image—essentially turning the image into black and white. If you slide the Saturation slider all the way to the right, you boost the color's richness—creating a day-glow effect. Last is the Lightness slider, which controls the amount of black and white in the image. If you slide the Lightness slider all the way to the left, the image turns black; all the way to the right, and it turns white.

One more feature I need to mention is the Colorize checkbox, which you can find near the bottom right of the Hue/Saturation dialog box. With this feature, you can load a black-and-white image, click on the Colorize checkbox, and wham, the black-and-white image takes on the color that you have set in the foreground color of Photoshop's color picker. So, if you had a bright red as the foreground color, your black-and-white image would take on a bright red hue after clicking on the Colorize checkbox. You might not want an overly saturated red image, but it gives you a good place to start because you now have some color to work with for what was previously a black-and-white image.

Now you're ready to look at some other things that you can do to black-and-white or grayscale images. Grayscale images are important because you'll use a lot of them for 3D. Three-dimensional programs use grayscale values to control bump, diffusion, specularity, transparency maps, and so on. Don't worry; I'll get into the specifics of the mapping techniques a little later. For now, concentrate on some of the ways that you can use Photoshop to manipulate grayscale images. One way is to use Brightness/Contrast.

Setting Brightness/Contrast

As the name implies, the Brightness/Contrast allows you to manipulate the amounts and concentrations of dark and light in an image. It's not limited to working only with grayscale images; it's also great for controlling color changes, but you'll concentrate on using Brightness/Contrast for manipulating grayscale images here. To get started, create a grayscale image from the Color layer of the Face.psd file by following these steps:

1. Open the Face.psd file if it's not already open.

2. Make the Color layer active by clicking on it.

3. Select Layers|Duplicate Layer. Rename the copy of the Color layer "Gray".

4. To make this a grayscale image, you need to remove all its color. Make sure that the Gray layer is currently active. Then select Image|Adjust|Hue/Saturation.

5. Move the Saturation slider all the way to the extreme left (-100). The Gray layer should now look like Figure 1.10.

6. Select Image|Adjust|Brightness/Contrast to open the dialog box. If you push the Brightness slider to the right, the image becomes brighter; to the left, darker. Think of using the Brightness slider as a way to add or subtract light from the image. The Contrast slider, on the other hand, allows you to add contrast by sliding it to the right or to remove contrast by sliding it to the left.

You'll be getting a lot of use out of the Brightness/ Contrast dialog in the upcoming tutorials. For now, take a look at a similar dialog box: Levels.

Using Levels

Although the Levels dialog box (Image|Adjust| Levels, as shown in Figure 1.11) is similar to Brightness/Contrast in that both allow you to manipulate the amounts and concentrations of darkness and lightness in the image, Levels gives you a wider range of control.

Levels contains something that looks like a graph with a slider beneath it. The slider has three little triangles attached to it: The one on the far left is appropriately colored black because it controls the blackness or darkness of the image; if you slide it to the right, the image gets darker. The slider in the middle, which is colored gray, controls the midtones of the image; if you slide it to the right, the image becomes darker; to the left, lighter. The far left slider, which is white, controls the white or highlights of the image; if you slide it to the left, the image becomes darker. Beneath these triangle sliders is another slider that is shaded from black to white. If you slide it from the far left to the right, you add more black (shadows) to the image. If you slide it from the far right to the left, you add more white (highlights) to the image.

The Levels dialog box is more flexible than the Brightness/Contrast dialog box, but not just because Levels has more buttons and sliders to it. Sometimes, when you're trying to get the contrast of an image just right, the Brightness/Contrast dialog box just doesn't do the job. With Brightness/ Contrast you can also increase the image's saturation, and as you bump up the contrast, you create an overly saturated image, which is usually not what you want. With Levels, on the other hand, you can increase the contrast by manipulating just

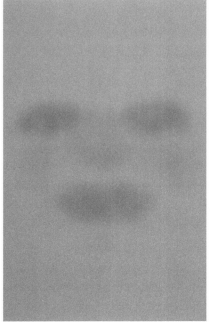

Figure 1.10 The Gray layer after removing all its color.

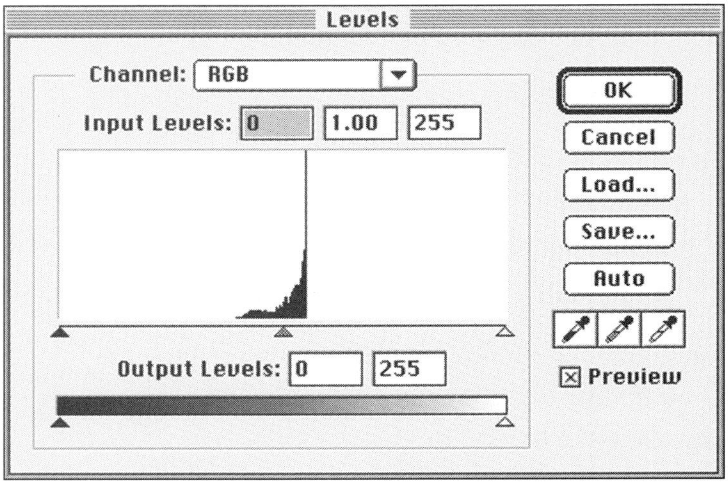

Figure 1.11 The Levels dialog box.

the dark (shadows) and the light (highlights) of the image without boosting the saturation.

Another tool in Photoshop's vast arsenal is the Eyedropper tool.

Using The Eyedropper Tool

Using the Eyedropper tool, shown in Figure 1.12, you can capture a specific color by clicking on the color that you want to use. If you double-click on the icon of the Eyedropper tool, the Eyedropper Options palette opens. By default, the Eyedropper captures the color of the pixel over which it's directly placed. You can increase this area in pixel size by choosing either 3 By 3 Average or 5 By 5 Average from the Sample Size pop-up menu.

Speaking of the Airbrush and Paintbrush tools, just what is the difference in the types of marks that these two brushes can make?

The Difference Between The Airbrush And Paintbrush Effects

You may think that the Airbrush and Paintbrush are pretty much the same tools with different names, but they're not. You can see the main difference between them by performing this little test:

Note: You can access the Eyedropper tool while you're using either the Paintbrush or the Airbrush tools by holding down the Option key (Mac) or the Ctrl key (Windows).

1. Press the D key on your keyboard to select the Default colors (black in the foreground and white in the background).

2. Create a new file by selecting File|New, and set the Width to 500 pixels and the Height also to 500 pixels.

3. Select the Airbrush tool, and give it the following settings:

   • Pressure: 40%

   • Diameter: 45 Pixels

   • Hardness: 0%

   • Spacing: 25%

   • Default Angle and Roundness

4. Make some marks with the Airbrush, making sure that you go back over your marks as shown in Figure 1.13.

5. Select the Paintbrush tool, and give it the exact same settings that you gave the Airbrush in Step 3.

6. Create some marks with the Paintbrush, being sure to overlap your original Paintbrush marks as shown in Figure 1.14.

Figure 1.12 The Eyedropper.

As you can see, the two tools make pretty different marks even with the same brush settings. Notice the difference particularly where the marks are overlapped with each tool. Notice how the Paintbrush makes the gray paint look as if the strokes are layered one on top of the other where

Figure 1.13 Creating some overlapping marks with the Airbrush tool.

Figure 1.14 The Paintbrush marks.

they overlap. The Airbrush, on the other hand, tends to darken the original strokes where you went back over them. Knowing the difference between the two brushes makes it easier to know when to choose the right brush for the right job or type of paint stroke that you want.

Moving On

Now you've reviewed the basics. I'll cover more advanced painting concepts in the next chapter, but the basics can get you pretty far when you're creating image maps.

ADVANCED PAINTING
TECHNIQUES
2

This chapter will give you a road map to some of Photoshop's more powerful yet difficult-to-understand features. After all, the program is so vast, mastering all of its features could reasonably take a lifetime.

A man once told me he had run Photoshop but couldn't get anywhere with it. It's a mystery. I can see how people might have this problem. One of the things that I love about Photoshop is its clean, unobtrusive interface, but at times, I can see how the sparse interface might be confusing to someone who's unfamiliar with computers or hasn't read much of the Photoshop manual. Some people pride themselves on never having read the manual for a certain program. Not reading the support material, to me, is like going on a long trip without a road map. Sure, you can get from here to there, but doing so will probably take you three times longer than it would with the aid of the road map.

Since you're reading this book, you're probably the type of person who is willing to do the extra work to learn some of the less obvious aspects of the software. In this chapter, I'll cover some of Photoshop's less obvious but extremely powerful features, including the following:

- The Smudge tool with Options
- Aging textures with the Burn tool
- Painting with the Clone tool
- Creating complex textures with fractals

The only problem in drawing with a mouse is that it's similar to drawing with a rock. Any artist will tell you that, if you must learn to draw with a rock, you learn to draw with a rock and become good at it. Drawing tablets can give you a much more fluid line. I've got one, but oddly enough, I end up using the mouse/rock more often than not. Luckily, you can use Photoshop, which does its best in making the digital drawing and painting process as natural as possible.

Using The Smudge Tool With Options

I know it sounds funny, but the Smudge tool was one of the main reasons I first purchased Adobe Photoshop. This tool has a great natural, human feel to it, and it makes painting with pixels a much more pleasurable experience. The Smudge tool allows you to blend, erase, and even paint certain areas of a drawing or painting that would be otherwise difficult or impossible with traditional media. In Figure 2.1, you can see a sketch I'll use as an example to demonstrate some of the Smudge tool's capabilities.

This figure shows a rough sketch called TV Watchers that I scanned into Photoshop. It was drawn in pencil on a piece of 8.5"×11" paper. Creating

Figure 2.1   The TV Watchers.

a decent sketch from start to finish solely in Photoshop is pretty difficult. You can, however, utilize Photoshop's advantages over the pencil-and-paper approach to perfect the drawing. This image is provided for you on the CD. To get started, open the file TVwatchers.psd in chapt2.

The Smudge tool is represented by the icon of a pointing finger in the toolbox. By default, the Smudge tool is set to Normal, which allows you to push or pull the pixels lying directly beneath the tool when you click and hold down the mouse button. Most of the time, the Normal setting works just fine, but sometimes you might want to constrain the tool's capabilities. When you double-click on the icon, the Smudge tool Options palette opens, as shown in Figure 2.2.

Here, you can choose from several options: Normal, Darken, Lighten, Hue, Saturation, Color, and Luminosity. Because the sketch is a grayscale image, the Hue, Saturation, Color, and Luminosity are unavailable for the selection right now. Figure 2.3 shows a section of the image in which the jaw line of the character's face can be seen through his fingers—as though the fingers were semitransparent.

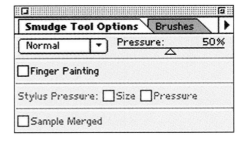

Figure 2.2   The Smudge Tool Options palette.

A problem like this can be pretty difficult to fix with a regular eraser, but by using the Smudge tool, you can solidify those fingers fairly easily. Set the Smudge Tool Options to Lighten and the Pressure to 76%. For the brush size, use the following settings:

- Diameter: 5 pixels

- Hardness: 0%

- Spacing: 10%

- Default Angle and Roundness

Use the Smudge tool as though it were an eraser, and remove the jaw line that can be seen through two of the fingers. The results should match Figure 2.4.

Similarly, you can use the Smudge tool to soften certain areas like the shadows on the Egyptian figure's head shown in Figure 2.5.

All you need to do is double-click on the Smudge tool in the toolbox and apply these settings:

- Darken

- Pressure: 50%

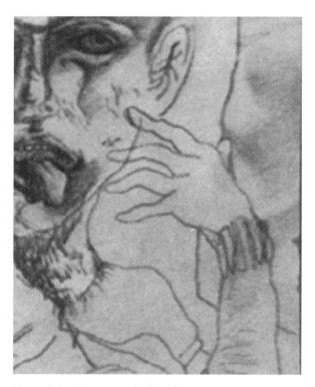

Figure 2.3 Transparent-looking fingers.

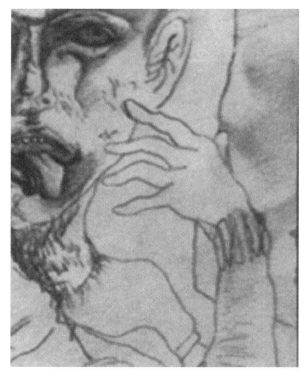

Figure 2.4 After removing the jaw line with the Smudge Tool.

- Diameter: 13 pixels

- Hardness: 0%

- Spacing: 1%

- Default Angle and Roundness

Using forward and backward strokes, rub along the outer edge of the shadow area. The results should look like Figure 2.6.

As you can see, by experimenting with the Smudge Options, you can gain a great deal of control over particular areas in your image maps. Be sure to experiment with some of the other settings such as Hue, Saturation, Color, and Luminosity on a color image. You can use the Smudge tool like a paintbrush, but by using the options available, you can create certain effects that would be unimaginable with a normal, nondigital paintbrush.

Now, take a look at another one of Photoshop's incredibly useful tools—the Burn tool.

Aging Textures With The Burn Tool

The Burn tool gets its name from traditional photography. In photography, if you want to make a specific area of an image darker, you need to expose that area longer while in the darkroom. Usually, you

Figure 2.5 The Egyptian figure before softening its shadows.

Figure 2.6 The shadow area after softening it with the Smudge tool.

Note: *I'll explain how to create the leaf image map in Chapter 11.*

do so by cutting a hole in a piece of cardboard and lining up the hole over the area of the final print that you want darkened while exposing the image. Photoshop makes this process somewhat easier because you can literally paint in the areas that you want to darken by using the Burn tool. However, you needn't think of the Burn tool as being merely a darkening tool. When you're working with color images, the Burn tool also makes colors more saturated where it is applied. To demonstrate some of the effects you can achieve with the Burn tool, open a color image map for a leaf and add some age to it.

1. From the companion CD, open the file called Leaf.psd, which you can find in chapt2\Burn. Here, you have a simple, two-color painting for a leaf color map, as shown in Figure 2.7.

2. Double-click on the Burn tool icon to open its options. The Burn tool icon looks like a hand pinching something.

3. Apply the following settings for the Burn tool:

   • Midtones

   • Exposure: 34%

   • Diameter: 35 pixels

   • Hardness: 0%

   • Spacing: 25%

   • Default Angle and Roundness

Figure 2.7   The leaf image before aging (see figure in Color Studio).

Figure 2.8   The aged color map for the leaf (see figure in Color Studio).

4. With the Burn tool, paint along the light green lines of the leaf, as shown in Figure 2.8.

As you can see, adding a little age or variation to an image's color can be quick and easy with the Burn tool. Using this tool is also a great way to add dirt and age to walls, spaceships, wood, cloth, plastics—nearly anything that you want to add some chaotic color variation.

Next, take a look at one of Photoshop's most useful duplicating tools—the Clone tool.

Painting With The Clone Tool

Not only will the Clone tool save you hours of work, but it can also save you from doing a lot of tedious, repetitive painting operations, such as painting thousands of whiskers onto a 3D character's face.

Figure 2.9 shows the color map for a 3D character's face. Because this image is going to be a rather grizzled 3D character, you should add some whiskers to his face.

1. Open the file called Face.psd, which you can find in the chapt2 folder on the CD.

2. To get started, add a few whiskers to the character's chin area. To do so, create a light gray whisker color, RGB 218, 218, 218.

3. Double-click on the Paintbrush icon to open the Paintbrush Options palette, and give it the following settings:

   • Normal

   • Pressure: 74%

   • Diameter: 1 pixel

   • Hardness: 100%

   • Spacing: 10%

   • Default Angle and Roundness

Figure 2.10 shows what the whiskers should resemble at this point.

4. Double-click on the Clone tool to bring up its Options palette. Apply the following settings:

   • Normal

   • Opacity: 100%

   • Option: Clone (Non Aligned)

   • Diameter: 27 pixels

   • Hardness: 0%

   • Spacing: 25%

   • Default Angle and Roundness

5. Move the Clone tool cursor over the whisker area that you want to clone. Holding down the Option key (Mac) or Alt key (Windows), click once with the mouse. Clicking stores the whisker section into the Clone tool's memory.

6. Holding down the mouse button, paint where you want more whiskers to appear on the character's face. You might need to use short dabs at first until a larger area of whiskers is built up. After you've got a somewhat concentrated area of whiskers built up, don't be afraid to reclone this area so that you don't need to make so many short dabs with mouse. The whiskers should look like Figure 2.11 when you're done.

By using this cloning technique, you've just saved yourself at least an hour's worth of tedious whisker painting. Getting the feel of the Clone tool may take some time, but if you make a mistake, simply reopen the Face.psd file from the CD-ROM and start again.

Now, you're ready to move on to a little-known Photoshop filter that actually generates fractals—the Clouds filter.

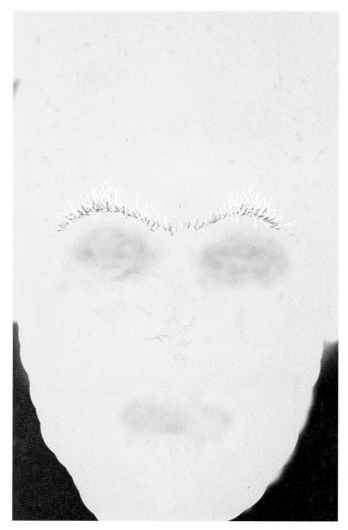

Figure 2.9 The color map for a face without the whiskers (see figure in Color Studio).

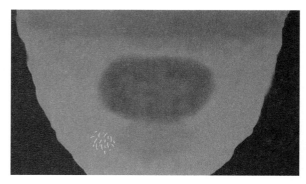

Figure 2.10 The character's chin after adding a few whiskers.

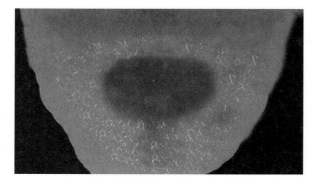

Figure 2.11 The completed whiskers on the character's face.

Creating Complex Textures With Fractals

Although the Clouds filter is great for creating cloud textures, it is actually very useful for much more. I've found it most helpful for creating a fractal pattern that can be used as a base upon which I can apply other filter effects to form water, rock, dirt, rust, and virtually any texture that exists. To better understand the fractal-generating effects of the Clouds filter, you should put it to use.

Controlling Fractal Effects

1. Create a new file that's 400×400 pixels square with a white background.

2. Press the D key on the keyboard to set the colors to default: black in the foreground and white in the background. If you had red in the foreground layer, the clouds would be red. I usually find it simpler to work with black-and-white textures to begin with and then adjust the color of the image later.

3. Select Filter|Render|Clouds to generate a cloudy-looking fractal pattern, as shown in Figure 2.12. Before moving on, save the file as Fractals.psd because you'll be using this file as your experimental, template image while using foreground color differences to show the changes in the fractal patterning effects that the foreground color can affect.

Figure 2.12 An image after applying the clouds filter (see figure in Color Studio).

4. To control how the fractal patterns are formed initially, use the color in the foreground layer and the Filter|Render|Difference Clouds effect. For instance, if you use a dark green color, RGB 5, 106, 0, in the foreground layer and then select Filter|Render| Difference Clouds, you get an effect like that shown in Figure 2.13.

5. Select Image|Adjust|Hue/Saturation. In the dialog box, move the Saturation slider all the way down to -100. The color of the image map is then removed, leaving you with a grayscale image map that can be used as a displacement map when you're generating terrain. I'll get into creating displacement maps in Chapter 12.

6. To further emphasize how the foreground color can influence the patterning of fractals when using the Filter|Render|Difference Clouds effect, change the foreground color to a light blue, RGB 62, 169, 199.

7. Apply the Difference Clouds filter. The results should resemble Figure 2.14.

So now you know that creating a variety of complex fractal patterns centers around the use of a specific foreground color and using the Clouds and Difference Clouds filters in unison. As I said before, using fractals is a great way to lay out a foundation image that you can alter using Photoshop's plethora of image-manipulating effects. Next, you can explore some of the ways these fractal patterns can be manipulated using the other Photoshop filters to form photorealistic image maps for 3D.

Figure 2.13 The beginnings of a good fractal displacement map for terrain (see figure in Color Studio).

Figure 2.14 Another fractal pattern generated by using a light blue foreground color (see figure in Color Studio).

Pushing The Fractals To Form Photorealistic Image Maps

1. Open the file called Fractal.psd that you created earlier. Use this fractal pattern as a base image with which you can create a photorealistic cracked rock pattern.

2. Select Filter|Stylize|Find Edges. This action gives you a grayscale image that resembles the look of hair or fur, but the image is a little washed out.

3. To remedy the washed-out appearance, select Image|Adjust| Brightness/Contrast. In the dialog box, decrease the Brightness to -2, and increase the Contrast to +94.

4. Select Filter|Noise|Add Noise. Set the Amount to 46, click on the Uniform button, and check the Monochromatic box. The result is a chaotic pattern, which in turn influences the Craquelure filter.

5. Select Filter|Texture|Craquelure. Set the Crack Spacing to 8, the Crack Depth to 3, and the Crack Brightness to 3.

6. Make sure that the Mode is set to RGB, not grayscale. (As you may have guessed, you cannot make any color changes to a grayscale image.) Select Image|Adjust|Hue/Saturation to add the final touch of color. Click the Colorize button on the bottom-right corner of the dialog box. Clicking this button turns the image to an overly saturated red hue, but you can change this setting. Set the Hue slider to 32, the Saturation to 39, and the Lightness to -52.

As you can see, fractals (or the Clouds filter) can give you some pretty elaborate patterns with which to work to form quick-and-easy photo-realistic textures. Be sure to experiment more with foreground color combinations to see how certain colors yield different fractal patterns when you also apply the Difference Clouds filter.

Moving On

Although Photoshop may seem daunting at first because of its sparse interface, with a little exploration, experimenting, and reading, you'll be an expert Photoshop jockey in no time. In the next chapter, I'll discuss some of Photoshop's editing techniques for creating 3D textures. So, take a breather, get a cup of coffee, and let's get started.

SPECIAL EDITING
TECHNIQUES
3

Because you're interested in creating image maps for use with 3D, a scanner is one of the most useful tools you ought to own, in conjunction with Photoshop and the 3D program of your choice. A scanner allows you to bring textures from the real world into your computer and apply a scanned image onto any 3D object's surface that you desire.

In this chapter, I'll discuss several important topics concerning scanners and the invaluable assistance they can give you when you're creating image maps for 3D art and animation:

- Choosing a scanner
- Working with scanned images
- Removing patterns from scanned images
- Using texture samples
- Removing items from scanned images
- Working with digital cameras

The significance of using a scanner cannot be understated, especially if you need to create realistic image maps within a very short time. Imagine, for instance, that you want to create the complex surface of the bark on a tree—with all its knots, chaotic color changes, rough texture, and perhaps even the markings of two star-crossed lovers. You could find a good photograph of a tree, study it, and then meticulously paint the bark using Photoshop's painting tools. This method could yield some pretty decent results, but it would definitely take you some time to complete—especially if you want photorealistic results. If you use a scanner, however, you can complete the job in just a couple of hours.

Choosing A Scanner

Scanners come in a variety of shapes and sizes and an even wider variety of price ranges. A scanner converts light into zeros and ones so that your computer can read and interpret that light. In other words, it transforms analog data into digital data.

Scanners use small electronic components called CCDs (charge-coupled devices) or PMTs (photomultiplier tubes) to see the image that you are scanning. A scanner divides an image into a grid and uses a row of eyes (called the scanning head) to record how much light is reflected in each location. After the computer has all that data, it builds a file representing the image in digital form. Each of the cells in the grid is called a picture element, or *pixel*. Scanners differ primarily in how many pixels they can measure.

The most common desktop scanners are like copy machines in that the item being scanned rests on a glass plate while the scanning head moves beneath the item. These days, you can choose from a large variety of scanners on the market. Flatbed scanners resemble copy machines. Sheet-fed scanners enable you to feed a sheet of paper containing text or art into them; these scanners are usually cheaper but give you a pretty low-resolution image in most cases. You also can find handheld scanners, which were quite popular until the flatbed scanners became affordable. Handheld scanners require a very steady hand and usually give poorer resolution than the flatbed scanners. The top-of-the-line is the drum scanner. This type of scanner usually costs tens of thousands of dollars but produces the highest resolution of any of the scanners.

Though each manufacturer's product will have a different "look," what really matters is how a particular unit measures up on the following counts:

- Resolution

- Bit-Depth

These criteria determine why one scanner will perform better than another.

Resolution

Although the concept can be confusing, *resolution* is a measurement of how many pixels a scanner can sample in an image. Resolution is measured by a grid. Think of a checkerboard, with eight squares along each side. The resolution of that checkerboard would be 8×8. If the checkerboard had 300 squares along each side, its resolution would be 300×300—the typical resolution of an inexpensive desktop scanner today. That scanner samples a grid of 300×300 pixels for every square inch of the image and sends a total of 90,000 readings per square inch back to the computer. With a higher resolution, you get more readings; with a lower resolution, you get fewer readings. In general, higher resolution scanners cost more and produce better results.

You can measure resolution in two ways. Manufacturers occasionally confuse the two in the hope of selling more products. Here's what you need to know about both:

- *Optical Resolution*—A scanner's optical resolution is determined by how many pixels it can actually see. For example, a typical flatbed scanner uses a scanning head with 300 sensors per inch, so it can sample 300 dots per inch (dpi) in one direction. To scan in the other direction, it moves the scanning head along the page, stopping 300 times per inch, so it can scan 300 dpi in the other direction as well. This scanner has an optical resolution of 300×300 dpi. Some manufacturers stop the scanning head more frequently as it moves down the page, so their machines have resolutions of 300×600 dpi or 300×1,200 dpi. Don't let these numbers fool you; what is really important is the smallest number in the grid. You can't get more detail by scanning more frequently in only one direction.

- *Interpolated Resolution*—You also should look out for claims about interpolated (or enhanced) resolution. Unlike optical resolution, which measures the number of pixels that a scanner can see, interpolated resolution measures how many pixels the scanner can guess at. Through a process called *interpolation*, the scanner turns a 300×300 dpi scan into a 600×600 dpi scan by inserting new pixels in between the old ones, and guessing at what light reading it would have sampled in that spot had it been there. In other words, the scanner inserts an in-between value based on the colors of the two adjacent pixels. The results are seldom satisfactory. Interpolation should therefore be avoided.

When you're thinking of buying a scanner, the cost tends to go up as resolution goes up. If you want to scan images that will appear in print, you'll probably want a pretty high resolution scanner (such as 600 to 1,200 dpi). However, if you'll be using your scanner mainly for creating 3D art and Web page graphics, the standard 300 dpi should suit your needs quite well because 72 dpi is the maximum resolution for most monitors.

Bit-Depth

The simplest kind of scanner, which records only black and white, is known as a 1-bit scanner because each bit can express two values, on and off. To see the many tones in between black and white, a scanner needs to be at least 4-bit (for up to 16 tones) or 8-bit (for up to 256 tones). The higher the scanner's bit-depth, the more colors it can see when it looks at any given pixel. As a rule, the higher the bit-depth, the higher the quality of the scan. When you scan images for 3D, you'll want a color scanner that's at least 24-bit. It will give you 16 million colors and a pretty high-quality image. You can purchase a scanner with 24-bit and 300 dpi resolution for a little over $100 these days. So, for just a few dollars, you can purchase a pretty high-quality scanner that can help you to increase the realism of your 3D images dramatically and at the same time save you hours of work.

Working With Scanned Images

Although a scanner can save you a great deal of time, it is not always the best tool for every texturing job. When you paint your image maps by hand, you have control over every aspect of the map because you created it from scratch. In what kind of situation would you be better off creating image maps by hand? In general, any time that you create the image maps for a face. If you were to scan the frontal view of a face, you would need to create a model for the face that matches up exactly with the scanned image map of the face. This approach really compromises your creativity because it is the image map that dictates what the final character will look like, not you.

So, when is a good time to use a scanner? There are no hard and fast answers to this question. However, in some instances, using a scanner makes more sense than creating the image by hand—for example, when you have time constraints that make painting the image map by hand impossible to finish on schedule, or when the surface that you need to create is so complex that your painting talents are simply not up to par for the task. Of course, even when you're working with a scanner, most likely you'll need to touch up the scanned image with Photoshop's painting tools.

Removing Patterns From Scanned Images

When you're working with scanned images scanned from a flatbed scanner, you'll rarely use the scanned image without any editing. For one thing, scanned images frequently have visible patterns in the image. Figure 3.1 shows a scanned image with these visible patterns.

You can remove the patterns from a scanned image in a couple of different ways. The easiest and perhaps the best way is to adjust your scanner's settings before you make the scan. Most scanners have a Descreen function with several subsettings for scanning newspapers, magazine images, or fine art prints. Compare Figure 3.1 with Figure 3.2. Figure 3.1 was scanned without using the Descreen function, whereas Figure 3.2 was scanned using the Descreen function set to Magazine.

As you can see, the image using the Descreen function looks much better than the same image without it. If your scanner doesn't have a descreening function, you can also use Photoshop's filters to remove some of the patterns from the scanned image. Choose Filter|Noise|Despeckle to remove the visible patterns occurring in the scan.

The number-one advantage to using a scanner is that you can choose textures from the world around you, capture them with a camera, scan the photos, and then apply them to 3D surfaces in your scenes. See the section "Working With Digital Cameras" later in this chapter.

Figure 3.1   A scanned image with visible patterns occurring.

Figure 3.2   The same image as Figure 3.1 scanned using the Descreen function on the scanner.

Using Texture Samples

When you're using scans to create texture maps, try to keep an open mind about how to use your scanned material. Just because you scan the texture of the palm of your hand doesn't necessarily mean that you need to use that scan to map onto the surface of a 3D hand. In fact, the skin texture from your palm can be used to create all kinds of skin or leathery surfaces. A scan of the rusty side of an old metal delivery truck can be used for the texture on the side of a spaceship or the walls of a dilapidated factory. Try experimenting with the scans that you create to generate a multitude of texturing possibilities.

As I mentioned before, you'll rarely use a scanned image as an image map without editing it at all. Most likely, you'll need to remove some artifacts from the scan.

Removing Items From Scanned Images

Figure 3.3 shows a scan that I made from a leaf of ivy. As you can see, the glossiness of the ivy leaf has resulted in hot spots of white occurring on certain areas of the leaf. Figure 3.4 shows the hot spots circled.

With the Rubber Stamp tool, you can eradicate these unwanted hot spots.

1. Double-click on the Rubber Stamp tool to open its dialog box.

2. Set the Options to Normal and the Opacity to 79%.

3. From the Brushes menu, double-click on a brush and set its Diameter to 35 pixels, its Hardness to 0%, its Spacing to 25%, and leave the Angle and Roundness at their default settings.

4. With the Rubber Stamp tool, sample darker portions of the leaf and paint out the hot spots until you get a leaf image resembling that shown in Figure 3.5.

Often, you'll find that the Rubber Stamp tool is a life saver when you're working with scanned images.

Working With Digital Cameras

Digital cameras have become quite popular in the past three years. With their popularity increase, the price has fallen. These cameras can range from about $300 to almost $10,000. A digital camera works pretty much like a scanner in that it uses a CCD to calculate light values and then turn those light values into numbers.

Figure 3.3 The unedited scan of a leaf of ivy.

Figure 3.4 Here, the hot spots of the leaf are circled (see figure in Color Studio).

Figure 3.5 The ivy leaf scan after removing the hot spots of the image with the Rubber Stamp tool (see figure in Color Studio).

The downside of using digital cameras is that none of them—even in the $10,000 range—come anywhere near the quality of a standard 35mm camera. However, if you're using the images captured from a digital camera for 3D or Web graphics, you really don't need 35mm quality.

The beauty of using digital cameras is that they provide direct access to images in digital form; no film processing or scanning is required. If direct access is your most pressing need and digital-camera image quality is suitable for your requirements, you can save time and money by using such a camera. If you already own a scanner and a regular, old-fashioned analog camera, you probably don't need to invest in a digital camera unless the time and money that you'll save in both film and developing costs make it worth your while.

Moving On

As you work more and more with scanned images, you'll find that they can be an indispensable in your 3D image mapping arsenal. When you're creating a background image in which the camera is locked down, you can use an extraordinarily complex scanned image to create unprecedented depth in your 3D scenes. A scanner allows you to bring surfaces from the real world into the realm of your 3D creations. In the next chapter, you'll learn how a 3D application allows you, the 3D artist, to map images (be they scanned or painted) onto your 3D creations.

PART II

IMAGE MAPS

IMAGE MAP
TYPES
4

The best way to create a photorealistic 3D image is to use image maps. People at MIT and many other technical institutes have been working on creating procedural textures that will dirty an object, but the results still come nowhere near the quality that can be achieved by an artist painting texture maps by hand.

A color image map alone usually doesn't look very realistic. The additional application of other surface attributes, such as specularity, diffusion, bump, reflection, and luminosity maps, is quite often required to create a truly photorealistic 3D surface. In this chapter, you'll learn about each of these image maps and their prospective places in the realm of 3D image making:

- Color image maps
- Bump maps
- Specularity maps
- Diffusion maps
- Transparency maps
- Luminosity maps

Color Image Maps

Often, 3D artists will create a color map (if they create an image map at all) and call it quits at that point. If the object is viewed from a distance, using just a color map usually is not a problem. However, if the 3D character or object is prominent in the scene, its realism quickly diminishes as you move closer to it. As with so many other art forms, 3D graphics rely on the suspension of disbelief.

Color maps, as you might expect, contain all the color information for the model. Because color is so psychologically powerful, color maps get a lot of attention. One thing you should avoid, though, is adding any shading or shadows to them. Your 3D program will take care of that job for you. Often, artists who come to 3D from an art background tend to add all these shading details when creating the color map. It is sometimes difficult to think only in terms of color and mentally remove all the shading information that light adds to form.

To make a surfacing job easier, it's generally a good idea to begin with a single, predominant surface color. This color acts as a base tone that you can work on top of—almost like laying down a base tone or underpainting when you're preparing a canvas for a work of art. After you find this predominant color, be sure to write down its RGB values. This base color will be the main color for all the color maps for each of the color sections that connect with it. Using this easy approach, you can avoid having seams because of color differences in your image maps.

Although you should not paint the shades of color (such as a shadow beneath a character's nose) that result from light and shadow in the color map, enhancing certain details such as wrinkles, pores, creases, and sharp folds can be helpful. These small details, which are really the result of shadows, sometimes need a little more help than just the bump map alone can provide. However, they must be shadow details that are so small you wouldn't notice something odd when the camera or the lights move. One of the advantages to adding these small details is that when you create the bump map, you can duplicate the color map and reuse those details without having to paint them again.

Bump Maps

Bump maps are extraordinarily valuable when you're creating photorealistic imagery. They are ideal for creating believable skin textures, wrinkles, pockmarks, scars, and many other small surface attributes that would either be too difficult or take too long to model.

Although bump maps don't actually change the surface of the model, they make light react to your model's surface as though they did. The principle behind bump maps is fairly simple: Dark areas of the map equal low altitude, and light areas equal high altitude—black being the lowest and light being the highest.

One way you can save yourself a lot of time and trouble is to simply duplicate the color map you've already created and use it as the beginning for the bump map. To duplicate the color layer, all you need to do is select Duplicate Layer from the Layers dialog box. You will then need to remove all of the color from the image by selecting Image|Adjust|Hue/Saturation. Slide the Saturation slider all the way to left (-100). You should now have a grayscale image that matches the color map. You can use this image to create a specularity map that exactly matches the details of the color map.

Specularity Maps

Specularity maps tell the surface which parts are shiny and which parts are dull. They are similar to bump maps in that they're usually grayscale images. Here's one exception: Rather than reading light parts of the map as high areas, they read light parts as being shiny. The dark areas of specularity maps are read as being dull or nonshiny.

Not all areas of any character's skin respond to light in a uniform manner. Even on undersea creatures, parts of their skin are more shiny or more dull than others. Just compare a fish's scales to its fins. Now, consider the human face. It's usually much more shiny around the forehead and nose area because these areas produce more oil and sweat than, say, the earlobe.

A fairly good rule of thumb to observe when you're deciding whether to make a particular area shiny is to consider how hard that surface is. How tightly packed together are the molecules that compose that surface? For instance, consider your own fingernail compared to the skin on the back of your hand. The skin is much softer and rather dull (not much light gleams off the surface), but the fingernail is pretty hard and therefore shiny.

Diffusion Maps

Why are diffusion maps the most misunderstood of all the map types? Well, for one thing, they are hard to define. Also, lacking a good definition of what they do, experimenting with them is hard because you may be unsure of how they're supposed to work. Often, artists take one of their previously made image maps and try it out in the diffusion map channel. For instance, say you take your bump map and drop it into the diffusion map channel. The result is that your 3D object becomes very dark. This result is no good. As a result, most 3D artists ignore diffusion maps altogether and crank the diffusion setting up to 100%. The result of this action is that something inevitably is not quite right with the final render of the character.

So, what does a diffusion map do? The best way I can define a *diffusion map* is to consider it as the final layer of your 3D object's surfacing. It's the final layer that light has to pass through before reaching the viewer's eye.

Are you totally confused now? Consider this: Light is the magical element that gives any object its color. Light comes streaming down at your character; it hits the surface of your character's skin, but not all the character's color bounces back at the viewer. Why? Because of diffusion. Most objects have diffusion. A mirror has a 0% diffusion, which results in none of the mirror's color being sent back to the viewer. Something like flat wall paint has about 98% diffusion. Skin, like that on most land mammals, has about 90% diffusion. When light hits a character's skin, most of its color is sent back to the viewer, but 10% of it is not. Figure 4.1 shows two creatures. The creature on the left has no diffusion map applied to it but the creature on the right has a diffusion map with the diffusion set to 90%.

Notice how the creature on the left appears to be flooded out with light while the creature on the right looks much more natural. This is thanks to diffusion mapping. The light settings are identical for each image.

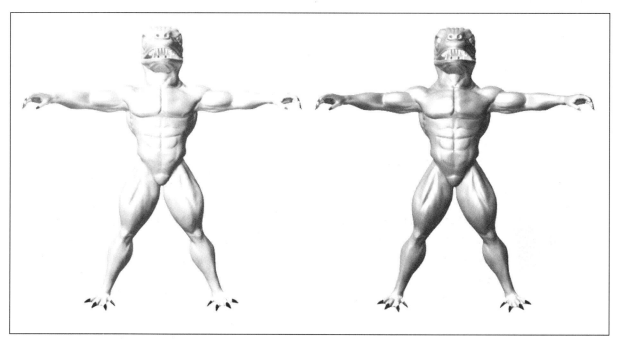

Figure 4.1   The creature on the left is shown without diffusion, while the one on the right has a diffusion map (with the diffusion set to 90%) applied to it (see figure in Color Studio).

Transparency Maps

Transparency maps (also known as *clip maps*) offer a great way to remove geometry without actually remodeling the model. A transparency map allows you to make areas of your 3D model transparent and/or semi-transparent by using a grayscale image. With most 3D programs, a white image map will result in none of the areas of your 3D object becoming transparent while an entirely black image map will result in the object becoming completely transparent or, in other words, invisible. By using various shades of gray, you can make areas of your object semi-transparent. Figure 4.2 shows a leaf that has been image-mapped onto a flat, single polygon square.

When the transparency map, shown in Figure 4.3, is applied, you get an image of the leaf without the extra geometry of the square polygon.

Using transparency maps is a great way to get the most out of your image maps and speed up rendering times all in one step.

Luminosity Maps

You may not use luminosity maps very often, but they offer a great way to add lights to an object when physically placing lights on the 3D object would be too time consuming or take too long to render. With a *luminosity map*, the black portions of the map give no illumination, and the lighter areas produce light. Figure 4.4 shows a luminosity map for the side of a spaceship.

Figure 4.2 A leaf that has been mapped onto a single polygon square.

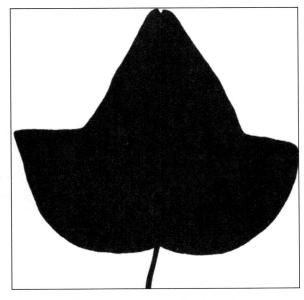

Figure 4.3 The transparency map for the leaf.

Figure 4.4   The luminosity map for the side of a spaceship (see figure in Color Studio).

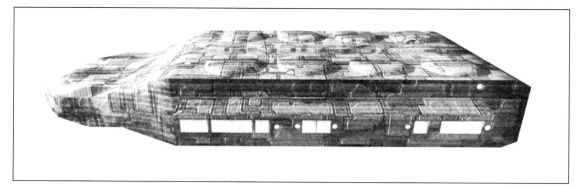

Figure 4.5   The spaceship after applying the luminosity map to its side (see figure in Color Studio).

After the luminosity map is applied to the actual 3D spaceship, the results look like Figure 4.5.

Creating Test Renders And Tweaking

Being impulsive by nature, I tend to apply each new image map to the model right after I create it. Using this same approach, you can immediately inspect your image maps. So, if the image map for the color of the front (even before applying any detail to it) is too dark or too light or too saturated or too whatever, you can fix it and get it right before moving on to all the following color maps. Also, this approach gives you an idea of what the color map will look like in the final render of the image. Another benefit of this technique is that it can push you in new directions that you may not have gone in if you were dealing strictly with the color map by itself. By allowing the image to evolve, with each render being a sort of incubation period between revisions, you can achieve a much more complete vision of how you want a character to look.

After you have all your maps painted and attached to the model's surface, you're ready to begin methodically scrutinizing how these maps interact with one another. This point can be both rewarding and humiliating, for it's the point at which you can see where the maps succeed and where they fail. Being as objective as possible is crucial at this point. Often, requesting someone else to lend a pair of critical, objective eyes can pay off at this stage.

With the model loaded into your 3D application, you now can go over it with a fine-tooth comb—creating close-ups and test renders of every conceivable view.

Often, rendering out animations of the model doing 360-degree rotations is helpful. These animations needn't be very long—maybe three or four seconds each—but they'll give the best indication of how well light plays across the bump-mapped and specularity-mapped surfaces. Change the lights and the camera angles around, and render the animations again, carefully studying the results.

Speaking of image map stretching, I recently learned of a great way to troubleshoot the 3D model to guard against stretching.

Guarding Against Image Map Stretching

After you select surfaces for mapping in your model (remember you did that in the beginning of this chapter), creating a small, tileable image map to be used as a surface tester is a good idea. This surface tester can be something as simple as a grid. Using this little surface tester, you can map it onto each of the predefined areas of the model.

After doing so, you can create some test renders and check to see whether you've got any stretching going on. Image stretching is an absolute no-no when you're creating photorealistic images. If you do find some areas that have image stretching occurring, all you need to do is go back into your modeling program and redefine the surface for mapping.

Unless you're part machine, you're bound to find problem areas in these stills and animations—areas where the maps don't line up quite right or where the nose is too shiny or the bump maps are out of alignment or where your maps are stretching. Tackle each problem area as it becomes evident to you. After all, this is the tweaking stage, so tweak away.

At this stage, most of the work has been done. In most cases, a problem exists only in a relatively small portion of the image map, so you can open the image map where the problem exists, fix it, and rerender the results until you're completely satisfied with your work.

The process of creating photorealistic image maps for a believable, 3D character seems like a long road, and it is. In the end, though, the results should more than compensate you for your labors.

Learning The Rules Of Surfacing 3D Images

I know that many folks—myself included—don't like a lot of rules impeding the creative process. However, I've found some basic rules to follow that can save countless reworkings and headaches when painting image maps:

- **Rule 1** *Avoid Using An Abundance Of Primary Colors*—Primary colors are pretty rare in the natural world; even the colors of flowers often become muted by the atmosphere, fog, and lighting conditions.

- **Rule 2** *Mirror Details*—Mirror complex areas to save time—not to mention your eyesight, which you'll need for more enjoyable tasks in the future.

- **Rule 3** *Remove Symmetry*—Order + Chaos = Reality. Mirror those complex areas, but avoid too much symmetry. After all, we live in a chaotic world.

- **Rule 4** *Avoid High Detail On Image Seams*—Avoid complex, highly detailed areas at the far edges of your image maps. Many details at the far edges of your planar image maps tend to run into the seam between the maps.

- **Rule 5** *Rely On Source Material*—Refer to your resource materials frequently while painting. Unless you have a photographic memory, keep those visual resources pasted right next to your monitor. There's nothing like the real world to clue you in when you're trying to paint something as realistic as possible.

- **Rule 6** *Perform Frequent Test Renders*—I render a test to check each and every image map as I create it. This step takes a little time, but it allows you to catch a small problem before it becomes a big problem.

- **Rule 7** *Fix Problems Immediately*—Fix any problem that pops up as soon as you notice it. It may seem like a drag to go back and fix little problems with your image maps, but the more problems you fix, the less likely they are to spread to your other image maps and pop up in the future.

Moving On

Well, I hate to leave you with a bunch of rules about maps, but following them will help you to achieve the high quality of imagery that you're after. In the next chapter, you'll learn how to apply these image maps to the 3D surfaces that you create.

WORKING WITH
IMAGE MAPS
5

One striking feature that separates a unique, drop-your-jaw 3D image from a mediocre, commonplace one is the quality of the 3D surfaces in the scene.

The surfaces of any 3D object supply the viewers with vital information about everything that exists within that scene. Usually, you want everything you create to appear to be tangible to the viewers; that is, the viewers should know what the object would feel like, what it's made of—if it's soft, hard, fluffy, dry, cold, wet, slimy, and so on. In short, the viewers should be able to relate the 3D object to the physical world. The best and perhaps the only way to make this leap is with the use of image maps.

How often have you seen an otherwise cool-looking computer generated model that just doesn't seem quite finished because the surfacing is poorly done? If you're like me, it's all too often. In most cases, you feel this way because the surfacing seems unrealistic and/or intangible. Often, the surface consists simply of a primary color, which looks like some kind of smooth, other-worldly plastic, and if the surface has any texture, it's probably a noticeably repeating or clumpy pattern. Such is the nature of default 3D shaders. If you want to create stunning, photorealistic images, you can't rely on default shaders because they simply do not have the detail and chaos that's required to mimic the details of the real world's complex surfaces.

Most 3D applications, from the $200 Hash program to the $10,000 Maya program, allow you to place scanned or painted image maps onto the surfaces of 3D objects. Using image maps, you can re-create the look of any surface in the real world.

Sounds great! But just how do you go about creating these image maps? To begin, you need to understand just how the image maps are applied to the surfaces of 3D objects before you learn how to create them.

Image Mapping Methods

The four basic types of image mapping methods are planar, cubic, cylindrical, and spherical. Every 3D application I've ever used contains at least these four. Each of these methods provides you with a way to get hand-painted or scanned images onto the surface of your latest 3D masterpiece. Often, you might need to use a combination of the mapping methods to get the exact look that you're striving for. Using these four methods, you can make your 3D characters, creatures, and/or objects magically come to life.

The Planar Mapping Method

As the name implies, the planar mapping method is great for placing a flat image onto a flat surface. For instance, if you have a model of a picture frame (with a plane inside the frame), and you want to place a picture of your good buddy Joe within that picture frame, you can use the planar image mapping method (see Figure 5.1).

This example represents an ideal situation, and as everyone knows, ideal situations are few and far between. Planar mapping is also great for mapping organic surfaces because it is one of the most straightforward of all the mapping methods. With planar mapping, what you see is what you get. Imagine that you want to planar-map the head of a 3D human character. You first need to break up that head into four different sections: the front of the head (that is, the face), the sides of the head, the top, and finally, the back of the head (see Figure 5.2).

You then need to make sure that each of the sections has a different color so that you can tell where one section ends and the other begins. Now, you can render out the four different views of your head model: a shot from the front, one from the side, one from the top, and one from the back. Using these images as templates tells you just what the boundaries of each of the four image maps will look like. So, for example, you can load the face into a paint program, select a new layer, and begin painting in the colors for the skin, lips, pimples, and so on. Using this method, you can ensure that the lips that you paint on the image map will exactly match the lips of the model—just as long as you crop the image map to conform to the face area of the model.

Figure 5.1 Planar-mapping to a flat plane.

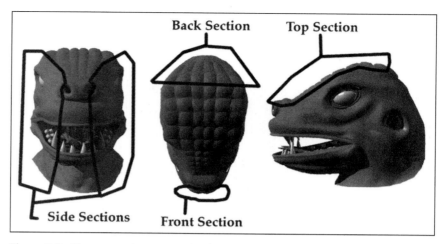

Figure 5.2 Planar-mapping an organic object.

A good way to think of planar mapping is to imagine that you are projecting your image map from a slide projector onto the preselected area (like the face) of the model. As long as both the image map and the preselected area have the same proportions, or the same ratio of height and width, you get an exact match of the features of the image map to the features of the model.

The only drawback with using planar image mapping on organic surfaces is that sometimes the image map stretches a bit in areas such as the nose and lips. You might get stretching in areas like the nose when you're planar mapping because the sides of the nose are nearly perpendicular to the front of the face; therefore, the image map has to stretch around the sides of the nose, just as if you were projecting the image from a slide projector. You can combat this tricky little problem in several ways; I'll get into them later in this chapter. Right now, take a look at some of the other image mapping methods.

The Cubic Mapping Method

Most of the 3D program manuals describe cubic mapping as a great way to map a box or a cube—which makes sense. However, cubic mapping is also a great way to map organic shapes. Take a look at how cubic mapping works. In Figure 5.3, you can see how the cubic mapping method takes the 2D image map of your buddy Joe and projects his face onto each of the six sides of the cube.

Using cubic mapping is a great way to continue repeating details like the windows on the sides of a skyscraper. I'll cover using cubic

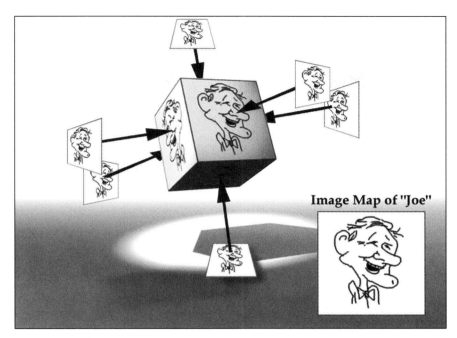

Image Map of "Joe"

Figure 5.3 Cubic mapping in action.

mapping for organic creatures a little later. For now, just let me say that cubic mapping is one of the most powerful methods around for surfacing creatures; it can save you a great deal of time and a bunch of headaches. Right now, though, let me talk about how cylindrical mapping works.

The Cylindrical Mapping Method

The cylindrical mapping method allows you to take an image map and wrap it around an axis. It's useful for tasks such as applying a label onto the model of a can of soda or for wrapping a texture map of wood around the model of a telephone pole. For an example of cylindrical mapping, look at Figure 5.4.

The Spherical Mapping Method

The last mapping method to discuss here is spherical mapping. Once again, as the name implies, this method is best suited for round objects. If you want to wrap an image map of the laces on a baseball onto a 3D ball or the continents of a planet onto a globe, you'd use spherical mapping. Spherical mapping is a lot like taking a big piece of paper and wrapping it around a beach ball—only without having to tuck in the edges at the top of the ball. Take a look at Figure 5.5 to get a better idea of how spherical mapping works.

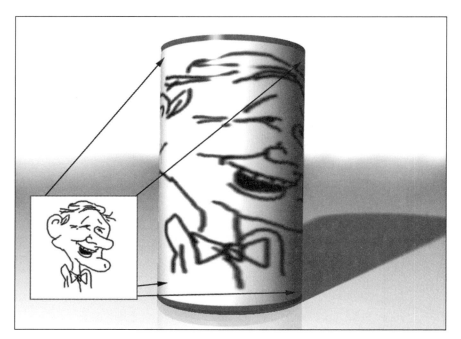

Figure 5.4 Cylindrical mapping in action.

Figure 5.5 Spherical mapping in action.

Working With The Mapping Methods

Now that you know the mapping methods, take a look at what you can do with them. For this section, you'll examine some case study images to find out just what makes a photorealistic 3D image. To begin, take a look at Figure 5.6.

In this figure, you see a simple cheeseburger on a plate with some fries. Looks good enough to eat, doesn't it? Everything in this scene—from the tabletop to the lettuce on the burger—is a surfaced and rendered 3D model. You might wonder why you couldn't just photograph a real cheeseburger on a real table. After the photo shoot, you could even munch out on the talent! For one thing, readjusting the scene after the scene's been shot and the set's been torn down is pretty hard. Also, a burger with lettuce and tomatoes doesn't look quite so appealing after it has been sitting under photofloods for eight hours.

With a 3D scene, you can go back and change the lighting, change the pattern on the plate, even change the texture of the sesame seeds on the bun. Best of all, though, the 3D burger needn't conform to the rules of the physical world. It can sprout eyes and a ten-gallon hat and begin line dancing if you need it to.

Figure 5.6 Burger and fries in 3D (see figure in Color Studio).

My main point is that 3D graphics have become so visually sophisticated that the line between reality and 3D has become seriously blurred. So, just how can 3D artists take advantage of these sophisticated tools and transport 3D models into the world of photorealism? Mainly, with photorealistic surfacing.

One of the defining characteristics of photorealism is to have a wide variety of surfaces. If you were to simply apply colored Phong shaders to everything in the burger scene, you would know what the scene was trying to convey, but you would be hard pressed to believe in its reality. However, if you were to use sophisticated image maps and seamless surfacing techniques, the scene becomes suddenly photorealistic.

Photorealistic surfacing results from a combination of artistic skill and observation—knowing what the viewers expect to see, and thoroughly knowing the tools that you're working with.

Notice the variety of surfaces that make up the cheeseburger scene. The bun looks soft and fresh, the cheese looks as if it's still melting, the fries look crisp and crunchy, and so on. These effects can be achieved only through photorealistic surfacing.

In Figure 5.7, you see a great deal of variety in the surfaces that contribute to shape this scene. From the leathery skin of the Sergeant Spore creature to the plastic abutment on the mop handle, you might

Figure 5.7 Sergeant Spore battling the Madagascar beetles (see figure in Color Studio).

think that this scene is real even though you know it couldn't be. Often, the little details of a 3D scene fool viewers into believing in its reality. Notice the attention paid to the surfacing of the Coca-Cola® bottle cap and the slightly reflective wood-grain texture of the floor tiles. These elements bring the reality of a scene home to the viewers because they're sure they've seen much of what is in the scene before.

The scene in Figure 5.8 offers a wealth of surface information for the viewers. Of course, a scene like this relies heavily on an abundance of 3D geometry and a variety of shapes, but that's not what makes it realistic.

If you check out the palm tree posts that make up the fence, you'll notice that each one of these posts is slightly different. A common mistake that 3D artists make is reusing a particular image map over and over again. Most 3D artists would handle the posts by creating one image map, cylindrical-mapping it around the post, and then using that map for all the other posts. This approach makes sense because it saves so much time, but it would really disrupt the believability of the scene. I'm sure that no two fence posts in the entire world are absolutely identical. I'm not saying that you need to make a separate, unique surface for each of the fence posts; doing so would take forever and also really bog down the machine when it came time to render the image. All you need to do is put a slight rotation on each

Figure 5.8   The jungle scene (see figure in Color Studio).

post and/or flip some of them so that you can hide the fact that they are all the same. That has been done in this jungle scene, and it really helps to keep the viewers convinced of the scene's realism.

The color used for this image is a concise color palette made up of dulled-down beige, yellows, and browns contrasted by the blue sky. It's not the type of color palette you usually see in a 3D image. Usually, you see the oversaturated primary colors that can be found in cartoons and package design. Primary colors are rarely found, though, in the real world. If the leaves on the palm trees in the scene were all primary greens, the reality of the entire scene would just fall apart.

Now that you understand the 3D mapping methods and have looked at some examples of photorealistic surfacing, you need to learn how you can prepare your models for the surfacing process.

Defining Surfaces

One of the most important aspects of achieving realistic surfacing is selecting the portions of surface properly. If you're not careful when defining 3D surfaces, image map stretching can occur.

Defining Surfaces For Planar Mapping

Image map stretching usually occurs when you're planar-mapping an organic, 3D object and the map begins to stretch around the curved surface. Figure 5.9 shows an example of image map stretching.

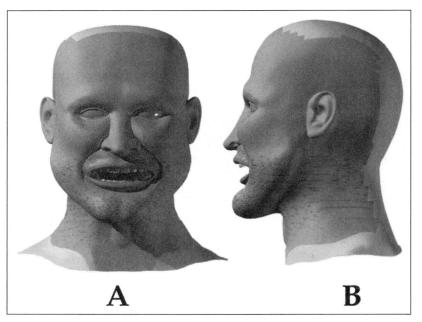

Figure 5.9 Image map stretching.

As you can see, the front face (marked with an *A* beneath it) looks okay, but the profile view (marked *B*) has a lot of image map stretching where the whiskers appear. The reason that the whiskers are stretching is simple: Because the image is planar-mapped onto the 3D face, the map stretches after the "plane" begins to curve too much. A good rule of thumb to observe when you're defining the surfaces for planar mapping is to try to select only the surfaces that exist on the same plane. Doing so can get confusing when you're dealing with an organic object like a character's face because it usually doesn't have any *actual* flat planes. By looking at the images of Gorg in Figure 5.10, you can get a good idea of where the safe areas or "planes" occur.

Testing 3D Surfaces For Planar Map Stretching

A good way to find out where image map stretching will occur is to create a test render of the object in question using a grid pattern that is planar-mapped onto the entire surface of the object. To create the test, just follow these steps:

1. To create the grid image to map onto the 3D object, use Photoshop to create a new file that's 50×50 pixels. Be sure that the file has a white background. (Press the D key on the keyboard to put black in the foreground and white in the background color layer.)

2. Choose Select|All.

3. Choose Edit|Stroke, and apply the following settings:

   - Width: 2 pixels

   - Location: Center

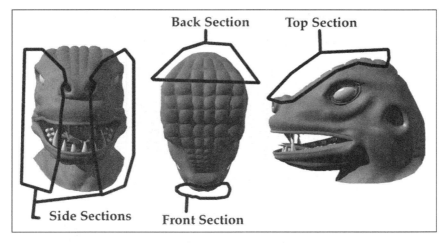

Figure 5.10 The selectable planes for Gorg's head.

- Blending

- Opacity: 100%

- Mode: Normal

4. Save the image as "Cube" in an image format that your 3D program can read.

5. Load the Cube image and the 3D model that you want to test for planar map stretching into your 3D program.

6. Be sure that all the skin of the 3D character is selected. That is, make sure that the top, bottom, sides, front, and back of your 3D character are all selected.

7. Planar-map and tile the Cube image map onto your 3D character.

    As you can see in Figure 5.11, the Cube image map shows exactly where image map stretching will occur.

Using the planar map stretching test, you can pinpoint the place where you need to break up the 3D model into sections; wherever stretching occurs with the Cubic image, you need to cut back on your selection of the 3D surface. If you look at the character's profile, shown in Figure 5.12, you can see that the front of the face is not stretching. This area is marked by two sets of dotted lines (the front of the face and under the chin) and represents the area that you would select for the front of the face if you were planar-mapping it along the Z axis.

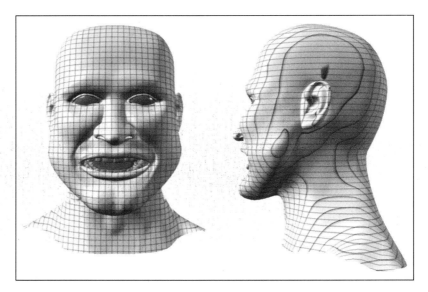

Figure 5.11 The Cube image map applied to the 3D model.

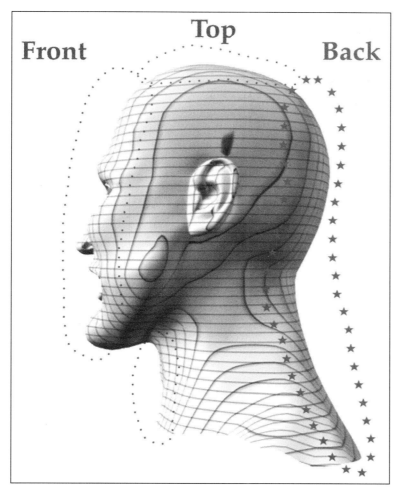

Figure 5.12 The areas that should be separated for planar mapping.

The area that is marked with the dotted line at the top of the head represents the part that you would select to planar-map the top of the character's head if you were to map it along the vertical Y axis. Similarly, the stars represent the selection area for the back of the character's head if you were to planar-map it along the Z axis and you wanted to avoid any image map stretching. By using the image map stretching test, you can save yourself a lot of time when you're preparing the 3D model for surfacing.

Moving On

Now that you have finished this chapter on how the various image mapping techniques work, you'll be getting into more tricks and applications of when and where to use these mapping techniques as you progress through the following chapters and tutorials.

USING LAYERED
IMAGE MAPS
6

Without the ability to layer image maps, you would have to resort to merging the information as layers in Photoshop. In some cases, this works fine, but in others it's a sad compromise.

In this section, you will learn about layering image maps—not to be confused with Photoshop's layers. Layering image maps is a feature found in many of today's 3D programs. This feature allows you to layer several image maps (for example, bump maps) one on top of the other. Although it may seem like a frivolous extra feature at first, it's not. Layering image maps allows you to create effects and surfaces that would be impossible to achieve otherwise.

To better understand the power and versatility that layered image maps can provide, work through this chapter.

Using Layered Image Maps To Texture A Shirt

You can layer bump maps to create texture for the front of a shirt. Take a look at Figure 6.1 to see the rendered model of the shirt you'll be working with.

The shirt has a color pattern on it, but there are no other image maps attached. To begin by adding a bump map, add the cloth's fabric texture to the shirt (how to create this particular texture is discussed in Chapter 10). After applying a repeating bump map fabric texture to the shirt, you will notice that the fabric texture alone is simply not enough to provide realism to its surface. This is obvious in Figure 6.2.

The shirt in Figure 6.2 looks as though it's been treated with a bucket of starch—it might make a good bulletproof vest, but not a very realistic shirt. What's missing from this shirt are wrinkles, which will make the shirt appear more flexible and light. So, what you want to do is apply wrinkles to the shirt and keep the fabric texture that is already there. Using the Burn and Dodge tools, you could create wrinkles over the fabric texture, as shown in Figure 6.3.

Now, if you were to planar map this bump texture along the Z axis and onto the shirt, the results would look like Figure 6.4.

In Figure 6.4, the wrinkles are too faint. You can hardly see them. If you want to make them protrude more, you could increase the bump map's texture amplitude in the 3D program, but then the fabric texture will become too pronounced, as seen in Figure 6.5.

As you can see, the shirt now looks like a sack of burlap—and the wrinkles still are not very prominent. This is why the layered image maps are essential.

You'll need to take a small, tileable section of the shirt fabric and make it repeat over the surface of the shirt with a cubic map. This

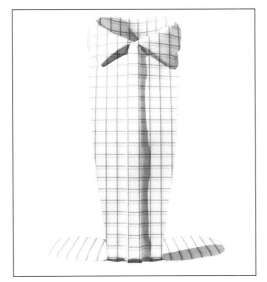

Figure 6.1 Rendered shirt with no texture maps.

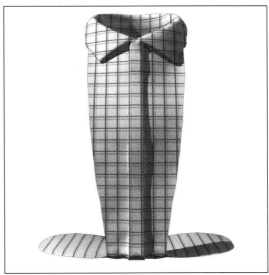

Figure 6.2 The shirt with a fabric bump map applied (see figure in Color Studio).

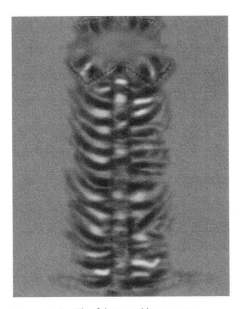

Figure 6.3 The fabric and bump map texture combined as one bump map.

Figure 6.4 The new shirt bump map.

saves the time of creating a very large image map for the shirt fabric and also frees up some memory in your 3D application. Take a look at A in Figure 6.6. This little swatch of fabric can be seamlessly repeated (tiled) over the shirt surface. B in Figure 6.6 shows a copy of the bump map shown in A with some changes made to it using Brightness/Contrast to create a diffusion map that can also be seamlessly tiled.

Figure 6.5 The bump map with increased amplitude.

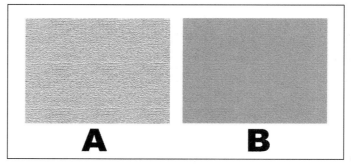

Figure 6.6 The tileable bump (A) and diffusion map (B) for the shirt's fabric.

Now, you just need to create another bump map designed specifically to create the wrinkles for the shirt, as shown in Figure 6.7.

Apply the image maps to separate bump map layers in your 3D program, and the results should look like Figure 6.8.

The shirt in Figure 6.8 sure looks a lot better than the ones in Figures 6.4 and 6.5. The only way to achieve the degree of realism that can be seen in Figure 6.8 is by layering the image maps. If your 3D program

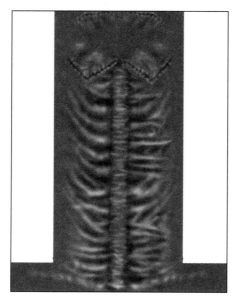

Figure 6.7 The wrinkle bump map for the shirt.

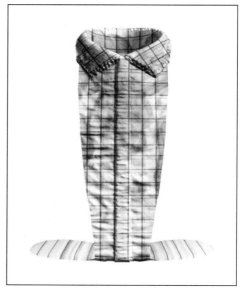

Figure 6.8 The final render of the layered shirt.

doesn't support them, tell the manufacturer that you want to see layered image maps as an option in the next upgrade!

Now, let's look at another situation where having the ability to layer your image maps allows us to create surface effects that would be impossible to achieve otherwise.

The Scale Problem With Gorg

In Figure 6.9, you can see the basic model of Gorg. You'll be getting to know Gorg a little better later. Right now, take a look at the naked model of Gorg.

Gorg is basically a cross between a muscle-bound human and a Uromastyx desert lizard. Because Gorg is a lizard, you'll want to apply scales to his entire body. This is simple enough to do if you use a seamlessly tileable bump map and cubic map it to Gorg's skin. Figure 6.10 shows the tileable bump map that was used for the scales.

When you take the scale bump map and cubic map it to Gorg's skin, you'll get something like Figure 6.11.

Just imagine that your clients said that they would also like to see some veins protruding all over Gorg's muscles. Now you have a problem. That is, you're in trouble if you cannot layer your image maps. You could try to planar map the scales onto the surface of Gorg's skin with the veins painted on top of the scales, but you'd run the risk of having a nervous breakdown trying to get all of those scales to line up

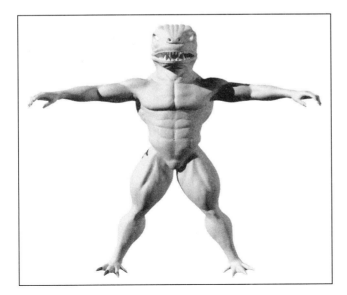

Figure 6.9 Gorg with no image maps applied (see figure in Color Studio).

Figure 6.10 The seamless, tileable bump map used for Gorg's scales.

Figure 6.11 Gorg with the scale bump map applied.

exactly with one another as planar maps. Also, it would take quite a few hours to create all of those scale maps with veins painted on them to cover all of Gorg's skin. The best solution to this nightmarish situation is to use layered image maps. Leave the tileable bump map for the scales as is and create a new bump map for the veins. Figure 6.12 shows the new bump map for Gorg's veins.

Add a new bump layer and planar map the vein bump. Figure 6.13 shows the results.

Now, the powers that be might decide that the muscles aren't quite as noticeable as they were before all of those scales and veins were added to Gorg and they want the muscles to be enhanced further with an additional bump map. No problem, you simply need to create yet another bump map to layer on top of the others. This layer enhances Gorg's musculature. Take a look at Figure 6.14 to see the third bump map created for Gorg's sinews. Figure 6.15 shows what Gorg looks like with all three bump maps layered onto his skin.

As you can see, you can exercise a great deal of control over the model by using layered image maps. If you take a careful look and compare Figure 6.13 with Figure 6.15, you'll notice that it seems some of the veins are now missing from Gorg's chest and leg areas. The reason for this is that when you layer image maps they can cancel each other out, which brings you to the next step.

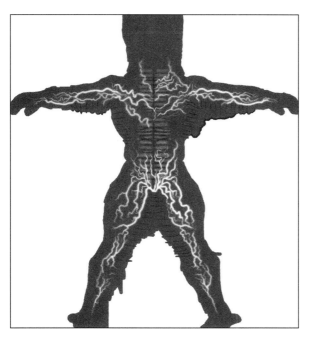

Figure 6.12   The vein bump map for Gorg.

Figure 6.13   Gorg with the layered scale and vein bump maps (see figure in Color Studio).

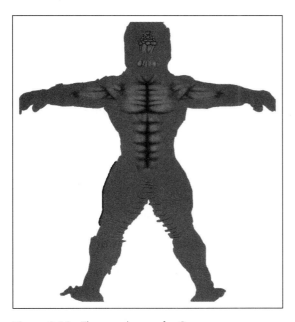

Figure 6.14   The muscle map for Gorg.

Figure 6.15   Gorg with all three bump maps applied.

How Layered Image Maps Can Cancel One Another Out

Take a look at Figure 6.16 and note the bump map of the letter A.

Because it's dark, the letter would cause an indentation on the model it's applied to, as illustrated in Figure 6.17.

There—that looks like the A pushed into the plane. Now, take a look at Figure 6.18, which is the negative of Figure 6.16.

If you apply Figure 6.18 to the plane as a bump map, the result looks like Figure 6.19. As you would expect, the A is now protruding from the plane. The funny thing is that if you layer the black A over the white A and give them both the same texture amplitudes in your 3D program, the two cancel one another out leaving you with a flat, blue plane. This is something to watch out for when layering your image maps. It happens with color, specularity, diffusion, and transparency maps, as well as bump maps.

The way to avoid cancellation is to layer the image maps in priority of the effect. For example, to create the three layers of Gorg's skin bump, you want to start with the muscles first, because they have the greatest mass. Then, you add the veins and finally the scales. This way the scales are the top layer, giving them the greatest strength. Because the scales are a small repeating bump map, they only slightly diminish

Figure 6.16 The bump map of the letter A.

Figure 6.17 The A bump map applied to a plane.

Figure 6.18 The white A.

Figure 6.19 The A protruding from the plane.

the effect of the muscle and vein bumps. The same applies for the veins. They have little impact on the muscle bump because they are localized on the surface.

Be sure that you always consider the priority of the effect when adding image map layers.

Moving On

Layered image maps can be used as bump maps, but they're just as useful when it comes to layering color, specularity, and diffusion maps. As you progress through the chapters in this book, you'll be introduced to some great examples and situations in which layered image maps become invaluable.

As an optional exercise, take a look at objects in the world around you as you go through the day and try to imagine how you'd re-create a particular surface. Ask yourself if you would use layered image maps and how you would use them to create the real-world surfaces you see. Remember, creating realistic 3D graphics involves at least 80 percent observation and only 20 percent creation.

PART III

TEXTURES

PAINTING INDUSTRIAL TEXTURES

7

When you create objects in the 3D realm, if their surfaces are unmarred and pristine, they look somewhat artificial. The reason for this is that when objects are used they tend to get scuffed up, chipped, or dirty. This chapter will show you how to add the mark of nature or humans upon items.

If you live in a big city, you'll notice that most of the surfaces you see around you fall into the category of industrial textures or surfaces. Industrial surfaces include all of those objects that are made by man. Man-made objects are essentially pristine when they come out of the factory or store. It's easy to simulate the pristine look of, say, brand new plastic with any 3D program. But it doesn't stay pristine looking for very long. Take a look around you and see that most of the store-bought, man-made objects nearby have been touched in some way.

In this chapter, you'll create industrial, man-made surfaces that look very realistic because of the influence of man and nature upon their surfaces, including:

- Dirt
- Chipped paint
- Layered paint
- Burn marks
- Rust textures

Adding Dirt To Surfaces

Dirt is everywhere. I don't care whether you're one of the biggest clean freaks this side of Felix Unger, dirt gets on everything. In fact, if dirt is not present on most surfaces, they will not appear to be real. Dirt is an often-overlooked characteristic of many of the 3D surfaces that you'll see, especially industrial surfaces. For example, look at Figure 7.1.

This car door looks fairly good if you were interested in getting a brand new, sparkling clean car door. However, if you want this door to look as if it came from the real world, where dust, sand, and road debris are constantly flying, you had better add some dirt. The type of dirt you add is an important topic.

The History Of The Object

As with anything you create in 3D—whether it's a character, a creature, or a coffee table—the object should appear as though it has a history. The object should look as though it belongs to the natural world that everyone occupies. To give the 3D character or object a history, you need to think of where it's been and who's used and/or abused it. How old or new is it? How was it was taken care of, and most important, what kind of impression do you want it to give the

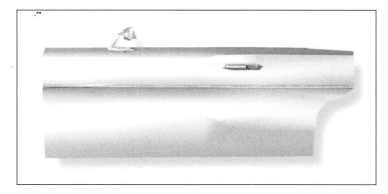

Figure 7.1 Dirtless car door (see figure in Color Studio).

viewer? I know these considerations may sound strange when you're preparing to surface a mundane object like a car door. However, it's mainly because the object is mundane or commonplace that you really need to take special care in giving the object character or history through surfacing.

Just think—you've probably seen thousands, if not millions, of automobile doors. You know what a car door looks like. Therefore, you're going to know when one looks out of place. Take a good look at some of the car doors around you the next time you're walking through a parking lot. Just be careful not to become so absorbed that you get run over! Notice the variety of stains, dirt, smudges, and grease marks. Notice how some cars are more reflective than others, how some appear to have more personality than others, and how some look as though they've been through World War III and back. Of course, the types of cars you see depend on whether you look in a salvage yard or an auto dealership. But that's just the point. The surfaces of something even as mundane as a car door can speak volumes to the viewer if the 3D artist is willing to sit down and think about a few things before creating the texture maps.

When you're ready to create image maps for dirt, you first must consider a few points, such as what type of dirt you want to add.

What Type Of Dirt Do You Want?

Cars collect a myriad of dirt, from street muck splashes on a rainy night to the off-road mud splotches caked on and extending from the wheel wells to the neglected look of sun-dried dust on the hood to the look of half-frozen gray slush that's collected on the quarter panels. You've got a lot to choose from, but for the car door I create here, I think I'll give it that off-roadin' look.

Preparing The Model Door And Adding Color Maps

To begin, you need to prepare the model for the application of the image maps. This process is fairly simple because the door is pretty much a flat plane.

1. Open the file called Car door.psd in the chapt7 folder on the companion CD. Notice the two layers, as shown in Figure 7.2: A shows a rough, rendered image of the door, and B shows the wireframe of the car door.

2. Create a new layer, and name it "Color".

3. Create a new color with these RGB values: 186, 117, 76.

4. Fill the entire new Color layer with this color by selecting all of the color layer and choosing Edit|Fill.

5. Select the Erase tool with the Brush Options set to Airbrush. Give the Airbrush the following settings:

   - Pressure: 12%
   - Diameter: 38 pixels
   - Hardness: 100%
   - Spacing: 25%
   - Default Angle and Roundness

6. Using this Eraser/Airbrush tool, remove the brownish color from most of the top portion of the car door until you see the layer below the rendered car door template.

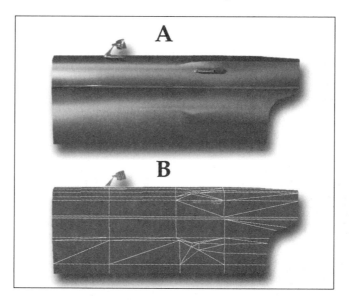

Figure 7.2 Templates for the car door.

7. Change the Eraser/Airbrush settings as follows to create a slightly smaller, softer brush:

   - Pressure: 12%
   - Diameter: 27 pixels
   - Hardness: 0%
   - Spacing: 25%
   - Default Angle and Roundness

   Using this new brush, touch up some of the mud areas, as shown in Figure 7.3.

8. Because the mud color is still a little too plain, select the Burn tool, and give it these brush settings:

   - Midtones
   - Exposure: 12%
   - Diameter: 35 pixels
   - Hardness: 0%
   - Spacing: 25%
   - Default Angle and Roundness

9. Use the Burn tool to darken the mud areas that are closest to the bottom of the door. Because this area is closest to the ground, the mud would be thickest here. If you darken this area, the mud will appear to be more wet (see Figure 7.4).

Figure 7.3 Touching up the mud with a smaller Airbrush/Eraser tool.

Figure 7.4 Darkening some of the mud.

Now that you've created the color layer for the mud, you still need to add the color or paint to the door.

Painting The Car Door

To add paint to the car door, you just need to follow these few simple steps.

1. Create a new layer and name it "Color2".

2. Select all of this layer, and fill it with the color that you want for your car door. (I chose RGB 91, 159, 213.)

   Notice that this new bluish color is a little plain. After all, you're trying to make this door look dirty.

3. Add a little dirt to the door's color by selecting the background color swatch (that's the one that lies directly beneath the foreground color you just created). Change the background color to a darker blue with these RGB values: 47, 87, 118.

4. Apply the filter by choosing Filter|Render|Clouds (see Figure 7.5).

5. Move the Color layer (the mud layer) so that it's on top of the Color2 layer. This way, you get a rough idea of what the mud will

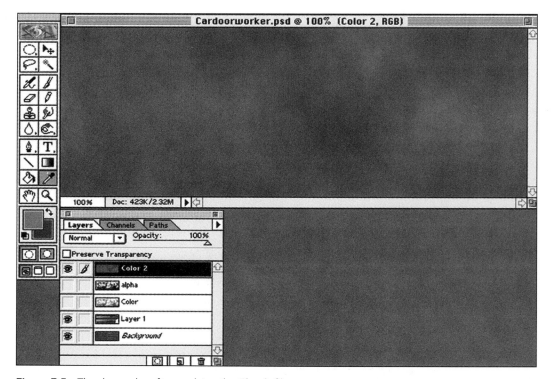

Figure 7.5 The door color after applying the Clouds filter.

Figure 7.6 The mud layer covering the door's color.

look like on top of the door's color. Link the Color layer with the Color2 layer, and select Merged Linked from the layers palette. The results should look like Figure 7.6.

Saving the file at this point is a good idea. The mud coloring is pretty much complete, but you still need to add texture, diffusion, and specularity to the door. To save some time in creating those maps, you can make a duplicate of the Color mud layer. If you were to merge the two color layers now, you would probably run into some problems later when you attempted to separate the mud areas from the blue door color areas. After you duplicate the Color mud layer, you can get started on the specularity map.

Adding Specularity To The Door

Because you know that the metal of the door will appear much more shiny than the dried mud, you need to create the specularity map accordingly.

1. Make another duplicate of the Color mud layer, and rename this layer "Specularity".

2. Select Image|Adjust|Hue/Saturation and reduce the Saturation to -100% and the Lightness to -100%.

3. To give this specularity map a white background, create another layer and fill it with white.

4. Move this new layer so that it lies directly underneath the Specularity layer.

5. Merge the Specularity layer with the new, white background layer that you created in Step 3. The Specularity layer should now resemble Figure 7.7.

6. While you're still working in the Specularity layer, make a duplicate of it, and name this layer "Bump". (You'll need this duplicate a little later.)

Figure 7.7 The Specularity layer after the merge.

7. Open the Brightness/Contrast dialog box, and change the Brightness to -100 and the Contrast to -72.

That's all there is to creating the specularity map. Now, you can move on to creating the diffusion map.

Creating A Diffusion Map For The Door

1. Make a duplicate of the layer named Specularity, and rename the duplicate "Diffusion".

2. Open the Brightness/Contrast dialog box, and change the Brightness to +100 and the Contrast to -18.

3. Reselect Brightness/Contrast and change the Brightness to +52 and the Contrast to +11.

You have now completed the diffusion map. Finally, you need to give the mud some texture by creating a bump map.

Creating The Bump Map For The Mud

1. Referring back to the layer named Bump, select Image|Adjust|Invert. Because 3D programs read lighter grays as elevation and darker areas as lower elevation, inverting the bump map creates elevations where the mud appears on the surface of the door.

2. Open Brightness/Contrast and change the Brightness to -100 and the Contrast to +56.

3. Choose the Magic Wand tool, select a Tolerance of 20, and be sure that the Anti-alias box is checked.

4. Select an area of black toward the top of the image.

5. Choose Select|Similar, then Select|Inverse. The result of the selection should look like Figure 7.8.

6. Choose Select|Feather. In the dialog box, set the Feather Radius to 5 pixels.

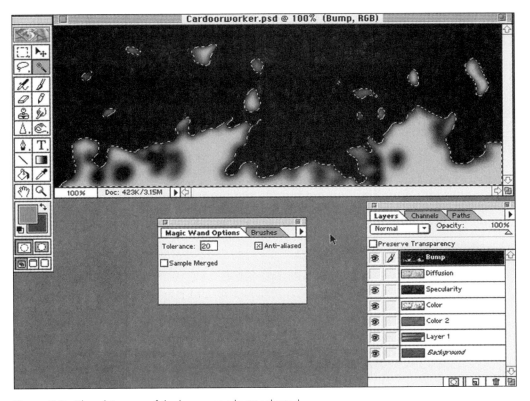

Figure 7.8   The white area of the bump map layer selected.

7. Select Filter|Noise|Add Noise. In the dialog box, set the Amount to 22, select Gaussian, and check the Monochromatic box.

8. To add a little more texture to the mud, select Filter|Texture| Texturizer; in the dialog box, apply these settings:

   - Texture: Sandstone
   - Scaling: 184%
   - Relief: 14
   - Light Direction: Top Right

   Also, be sure to check the Invert box.

9. Because the bump map layer still looks a little too harsh for use as a bump map, select Filter|Blur|Gaussian blur. In the dialog box, set Radius to .9 pixels. The results should match Figure 7.9.

Now that you've created all the image maps for the car door, you can save each of the maps as a separate file so that you can load the files into the 3D program and try them out. First, though, be sure to save the original Photoshop file.

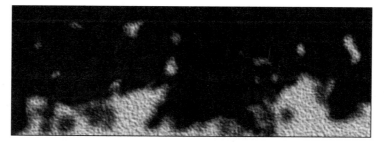

Figure 7.9 The final bump map for the mud.

Saving The Image Maps

To save the image maps, simply select all of the layer that you want to export, that is, the Color layer. Then, copy the layer, select File|New, and paste the Color map into the new file. Finally, flatten the layers and save the Color image map as "Doorcolor" or something similar in a file format that your 3D program can read.

After you've copied each of the color, specularity, bump, and diffusion maps and saved them, you can planar-map them along the Z axis onto the model of the car door. You can find the car door model in the Models/chapt7models folder on the accompanying CD. The door model is called "Car door", and it has been provided in various 3D formats, so just open the one that's compatible with your 3D application.

What The Dirt Looks Like On The Door

After you've planar-mapped each of the image maps onto the door model and tweaked the settings in the 3D program, you get something like the image of the door shown in Figure 7.10.

If you're not completely satisfied with the texture or the color of the mud on the car door, you can easily go back into Photoshop and mess around with the color layer or apply different filters to the bump map layer until you're completely satisfied with the look.

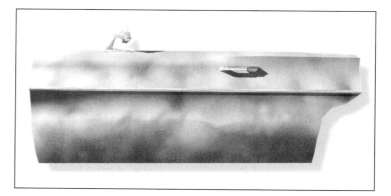

Figure 7.10 The final rendering of the dirty car door (see figure in Color Studio).

Now that you're experienced in creating digital dirt, you're ready to move on to another effect that you can apply to the same car door model: creating the look of chipped paint.

Creating The Look Of Chipped Paint

When it comes to creating realistic, industrial surfaces, being able to mimic the look of chipped paint is a must. Chipped paint gives the model the look of age and use. Many factors can cause paint to chip and peel: moisture; hot, dry climates; age; and physical use and abuse.

Image Maps Add Realism To Chipped Paint Texture

Adding the chipped paint look to a 3D model is next to impossible if you rely only on your modeling skills, but with image maps, you can create the look with stunning realism and accuracy.

Creating A Chipped Paint Color Map

Here's how to start the chipped paint look:

1. Open the file called Car door.psd in the chapt7 folder on the companion CD.

2. Create a new layer, and name it "Color".

3. Fill the layer with a light blue color, RGB 122, 184, 234.

4. Create another layer, and name it "C2".

5. Fill this layer with a red color, RGB 210, 35, 35.

6. Select Filter|Noise|Add Noise. In the dialog box, set the Amount to 56, select Gaussian, and check the Monochromatic box. At this point, the C2 layer should resemble Figure 7.11.

7. Apply the Craquelure filter with these settings:
   - Crack Spacing: 23
   - Crack Depth: 10
   - Crack Brightness: 0

Figure 7.11   The C2 layer after applying the Noise filter.

Note: *It's good to get in the practice of saving the Photoshop file and renaming it in stages. This way, you can go back to earlier versions of the file to rework certain areas if necessary. Also, with Photoshop 5, you can use the new Histories palette feature, which is an extensive improvement over the previously single Undo. With the Histories palette you can go back to any step that you previously created (depending on your preset cache levels and your hard drive space) and return to that point.*

Using these settings breaks up the red so that you can select the dark areas and remove them.

8. Select the Magic Wand, give it a tolerance of 1, and check the Anti-alias box.

9. Select the dark crack areas of the image, as shown in Figure 7.12. Choose Select|Save Selection. This way, you can select just the holes in the red paint layer later.

10. Press the Delete key a couple of times to remove the dark areas. You should be able to see the blue areas from the Color layer lying directly beneath the red C2 layer.

11. Change the selection by choosing Select|Inverse. You should now have the noisy red section of the C2 layer selected. Be sure that red (RGB 210, 35, 35) is the foreground color.

12. With only the red areas of the C2 layer selected, select Edit|Fill to use the foreground red to remove all the noisy red areas.

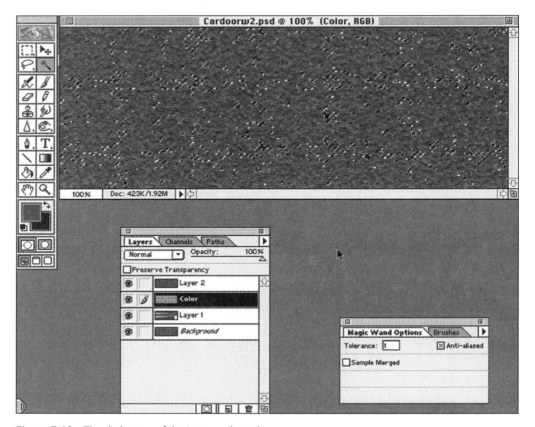

Figure 7.12 The dark areas of the image selected.

13. Make a duplicate of the C2 layer, and rename it "Bump". You'll be working on this layer in just a moment. For now, click the eye icon beside the new Bump layer so that the layer becomes invisible. Now is a good time to save the Photoshop file.

14. Make the blue Color layer active by clicking on it. Be sure that you can still see the reddish C2 layer on top of the blue layer. Select Filter|Noise|Add Noise. In the dialog box, set the Amount to 78, select Gaussian, and check the Monochromatic box.

15. Select Filter|Blur|Gaussian Blur, and set Radius to 1.0 pixels. This setting gives the blue C2 layer a little color variation.

16. Move back to the Color layer, and make it active by clicking on it.

17. Link the Color layer with the C2 layer; then select Merge Linked from the layers palette.

The Color layer is still a little too plain. You need to add a little more variation to both the blue and red colors.

Enhancing A Color Layer

You can quickly enhance your Color layer by using the Burn and Dodge tools.

1. Select the Burn tool with the following settings:
   - Midtones
   - Exposure: 32%
   - Diameter: 35 pixels
   - Hardness: 0%
   - Spacing: 25%
   - Default Angle and Roundness

2. Darken the color areas with the Burn tool (see Figure 7.13).

Figure 7.13 The Color layer after applying the variations with the Burn tool.

3. Change the Burn tool to the Dodge tool with these brush settings:

   - Midtones
   - Exposure: 32%
   - Diameter: 3 pixels
   - Hardness: 100%
   - Spacing: 25%
   - Default Angle and Roundness

4. Use the Dodge tool to create scratches across the Color surface. You can change back to the Burn tool (using a smaller brush diameter such as 3 pixels) to create some dark scratches.

That about does it for the Color layer, so you can move on to create the surface texture for the chipped paint.

Creating A Chipped Paint Bump Map

To create the surface texture, follow these steps:

1. Make sure that the Bump layer is the active layer. Select Image|Adjust|Hue/Saturation, and in the dialog box, reduce the Saturation to -100. This setting removes all the color from the Bump layer.

2. Apply a filter by selecting Filter|Sketch|Conte Crayon, and use these settings:
   - Foreground Level: 11
   - Background Level: 12
   - Texture: Sandstone
   - Scaling: 50%
   - Relief: 7
   - Light Direction: Top Right

3. After applying the Conte Crayon filter, select Filter|Fade Conte Crayon. In the dialog box, fade it 63%.

4. To take care of the holes in the Bump layer, create a new layer, and fill it with a gray tone, RGB 40, 40, 40.

5. Add some noise to this new gray color by selecting Filter|Noise|Add Noise. Set the Amount to 19, select Gaussian, and check the Monochromatic box.

6. Select the Bump layer again, and link it to the gray color layer that you just created.

7. From the layers palette, select the Merge Linked command.

8. Select Filter|Sharpen|Sharpen. The resulting bump map should resemble Figure 7.14.

9. To complete the Bump layer, add a little noise by setting the Amount to 26, selecting Gaussian, and checking the Monochromatic box.

Now that you're finished with the Bump layer, you can move on to creating the diffusion and specularity maps.

Creating A Chipped Paint Specularity Map

1. Make a duplicate of the Bump layer, and name it "Specularity".

2. Select Image|Adjust|Invert.

3. Select Image|Adjust|Brightness/Contrast. In the dialog box, lower the Brightness to -50 and the Contrast to -25. The final Specularity layer should look like Figure 7.15.

You've now completed the specularity map for the cracks. Finally, you just need to create the diffusion map.

Creating A Chipped Paint Diffusion Map

1. Make another duplicate of the Bump layer, and name it "Diffusion".

2. Choose Select|Load Selection. From the Channel area, load #4. This should be the selection of the holes that you saved earlier.

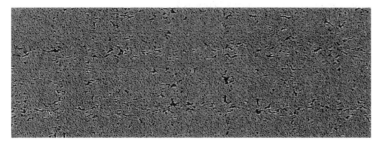

Figure 7.14 The effect of the faded Conte Crayon filter on the Bump layer.

Figure 7.15 The final specularity map for the chipped paint.

3. Choose Select|Inverse.

4. Select Image|Adjust|Brightness/Contrast. In the dialog box, raise the Brightness to +36, and lower the Contrast to -60.

5. Select Inverse once again.

6. Raise the Brightness to +40, and raise the Contrast to +6. The final Diffusion layer should look like Figure 7.16.

If your 3D program allows you to create reflection maps, you should add that extra touch of realism to the car door. You can make the door look as though the paint that has chipped off is revealing some of the reflective, bare metal lying beneath it. Usually, with reflection maps, lighter grays are read as being more reflective, and darker grays are read as being less reflective.

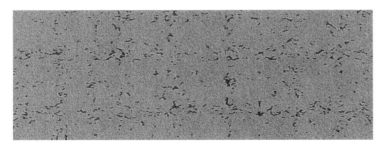

Figure 7.16 The final diffusion map for the chipped paint.

Creating A Chipped Paint Reflection Map

1. Create a new layer, and name it "Reflection".

2. Load the selection of the holes that you saved earlier in Channel #4.

3. Create a gray color for the holes, RGB 105, 105, 105.

4. Select Edit|Fill and fill the holes with gray.

5. Choose Select|Inverse.

6. Create a slightly darker, less reflective gray for the red paint area, RGB 10, 10, 10.

7. Fill the selection with this darker gray. Your reflection map should look like Figure 7.17.

Now that you've created all the maps for the chipped paint look, you're ready to start mapping them onto the car door.

Putting All The Maps Together To Create The Chipped Paint Look On The Car Door

Your first step is to save the Photoshop file. Then, select each of the Color, Bump, Specularity, Reflection, and Diffusion layers individually, and save each one as a separate file in a format that your 3D program can read. Remember to name each of the files so that you know which one contains the color information, which one contains the bump information, and so on. Map the color, bump, reflection, specularity, and diffusion maps onto the 3D door object. The final, rendered result of the chipped paint maps on the object should look like Figure 7.18.

Now that you've created some very realistic cracks on the car door, you can move on to a surface effect that is pretty similar but just as useful for surfacing industrial-type 3D objects: creating the look of layered paint.

Figure 7.17   The reflection map for the car door.

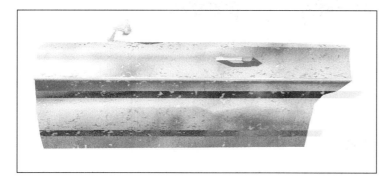

Figure 7.18 The final render of the chipped paint on the car door (see figure in Color Studio).

Creating The Look Of Layered Paint

Any time you paint over a surface in the real world, unless you meticulously scrape off all the original coat of paint, you leave behind evidence that this new layer of paint is not the original. The common practice is to scrape off all the original coat of paint that's peeling and paint over the rest. This process leaves the wall, dresser, or the car with an uneven, bumpy surface. It's a very common look for painted surfaces but very rare in the 3D world. For that reason, many painted surfaces in 3D lack realism. After this tutorial, you'll have no excuse for making that common mistake.

Maps For The Layered Paint Look

For that realistic layered paint look, you once again begin with color maps.

Creating A Layered Paint Color Map

To use the car door once again for this tutorial, open the file called Car door.psd in the chapt7 folder of the companion CD.

1. Create a new layer, and name it "Color".

2. Fill the layer with an ugly green color, RGB 52, 107, 64.

3. Select Filter|Noise|Add Noise. In the dialog box, set the Amount to 86, select Uniform, and check the Monochromatic box.

4. Select Filter|Blur|Gaussian Blur, and set Radius to 7.0 pixels.

5. Select the Add Noise Filter again. This time, set the Amount to 3, select Gaussian, and check the Monochromatic box.

That's all there is to creating the color map. The real fun starts with creating the bump map for the layered paint.

Creating A Layered Paint Bump Map

1. Create a new layer, and name it "Bump".

2. Fill this layer with black, RGB 0, 0, 0.

3. Create a new layer, and name it "C2".

4. Create a lighter gray color, RGB 51, 51, 51.

5. Select the Pencil tool with 100% opacity and a diameter of 27 pixels. With the Pencil tool, begin creating splotches of paint. Change the Pencil's diameter to 27 pixels, and add pointy edges to these paint splotches, as shown in Figure 7.19.

6. Create another layer, and name it "C3".

7. Create an even lighter gray color, RGB 150, 150, 150.

8. Select the Pencil tool again with 100% opacity, and a diameter of 27 pixels. With the Pencil tool, begin creating some more splotches of paint. Don't worry if you place these new splotches over the original ones that you created. Once again, be sure to change the Pencil's diameter to 27 pixels, and add pointy edges to these paint splotches.

9. In the layers palette, change the layer setting from Normal to Hard Light for the C3 layer.

10. Open the Brightness/Contrast dialog box. Change the Brightness to +20, and leave the Contrast at 0.

11. Select the original Bump layer, and link it to the C2 and C3 layers.

12. Select Merge Linked from the layers palette.

13. Using the Magic Wand tool with a Tolerance of 5, select the two lightest grays, as shown in Figure 7.20.

14. Choose Select/Save Selection so that you can load this selection later.

Figure 7.19 Starting the second layer of paint in the C2 layer.

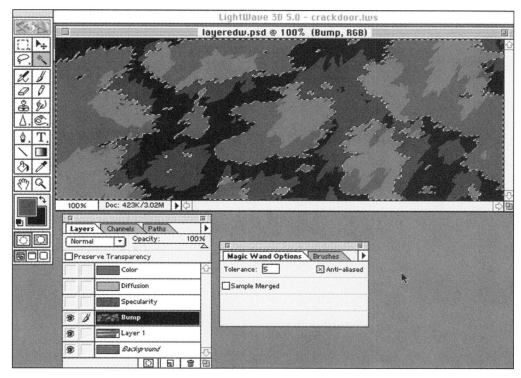

Figure 7.20 The two lightest grays selected.

15. Select Filter|Noise|Add Noise. In the dialog box, set the Amount to 7, select Uniform, and check the Monochromatic box. The results should look like Figure 7.21.

That completes the bump map for the paint layers. Now, you can get to work on creating the specularity map.

Creating A Layered Paint Diffusion Map

1. Make a duplicate of the Color layer, and change its name to "Diffusion".

2. Select Image|Adjust|Hue/Saturation. In the dialog box, lower the Saturation to -100.

Figure 7.21 The final bump map for the paint layers.

3. Select Image|Adjust|Brightness/Contrast, and apply a Brightness of +26 and a Contrast of +76.

These steps complete the work you need to do on the diffusion map, so save the Color, Bump, and Diffusion layers as separate files, and planar-map them along the Z axis onto the 3D model of the door. The results should look something like Figure 7.22.

You've nearly completed the tutorial for creating the look of layered paint. Now, you can move on to the next challenge, which is creating the look of realistic burn marks on paint and metal.

Burn Marks

Burn marks on objects certainly aren't as common as peeled or layered paint in everyday life. If you want to create 3D vehicles, spaceships, or robots that look as though they've seen some action, though, using burn marks is really the way to go. Once again, an effect like realistic burn marks adds to the history of the object. These marks indicate that the object has been through some tough scrapes but is still around for action.

Maps For Burn Marks

For this tutorial, you'll be using the car door once again as the object that's been through the fire. To get started, first create the color map for the burnt look.

Creating A Color Map For Burn Marks

1. Open the file called Car door.psd in the chapt7 folder on the companion CD.

2. Create a new layer, and name it "Color".

3. Choose Select|All, and fill the layer with a very dark color, RGB 6, 4, 3. It represents the color for the burned area.

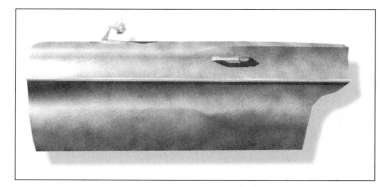

Figure 7.22 The final render of the layered paint look (see figure in Color Studio).

4. Create another layer, and name it "C2".

5. Create a much lighter color to represent the paint on the car door, RGB 229, 220, 200.

6. Using the Square selection tool, select about three quarters of the entire right side of the image, and fill it with the lighter color, as shown in Figure 7.23.

7. Create an Airbrush with the following settings:
   - Pressure: 12%
   - Diameter: 65 pixels
   - Hardness: 0%
   - Spacing: 25%
   - Default Angle and Roundness

8. Use this Airbrush to begin blending the far left edge gradually into the black area, as shown in Figure 7.24.

9. Select the Burn tool with these settings:
   - Exposure: 70%

> **Note:** You may need to change the Airbrush's size (diameter) a couple of times to create a less uniform fade into the black area. To do this, simply double-click on the Airbrush icon, select the Brushes tab, and then double-click on the current brush to change its brush diameter—or single click on a smaller brush and use that.

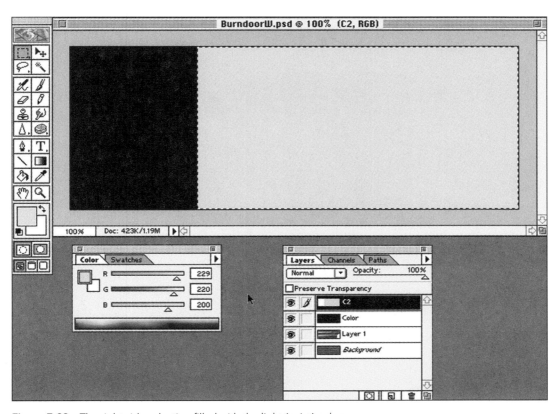

Figure 7.23 The right side selection filled with the light (paint) color.

Figure 7.24 The blended edge of the C2 layer into the black Color layer.

- Diameter: 65 pixels
- Hardness: 0%
- Spacing: 25%
- Default Angle and Roundness

10. Use the Burn tool to create a brownish color at the edge where the light-colored paint begins to fade into the black area (see Figure 7.25).

11. Create yet another layer, and name it "C3".

12. Utilizing the Lasso selection tool, create some peeled paint shapes, and then fill each one with a brown color, RGB 55, 36, 16 (see Figure 7.26).

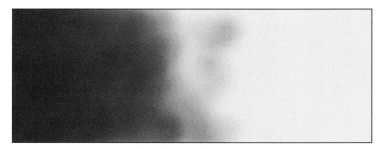

Figure 7.25 After painting the faded edge with the Burn tool.

Figure 7.26 The peeled paint shapes filled with brown.

13. Using the Burn tool, darken some of the areas on these peeled paint shapes in the C3 layer. Use the following settings for the Burn tool:

   - Exposure: 70%
   - Diameter: 35 pixels
   - Hardness: 0%
   - Spacing: 25%
   - Default Angle and Roundness

14. Switch to the Dodge tool, and apply a little more variation to the peeled paint shapes. (Use the settings in Step 13 for the Dodge tool, but change the Exposure to 50%.)

15. Select the Sponge tool with the following settings:

   - Saturate
   - Exposure: 67%
   - Diameter: 13 pixels
   - Hardness: 0%
   - Spacing: 25%
   - Default Angle and Roundness

   Use the Sponge tool to add some orange to the shapes. Figure 7.27 shows the results of the Burn, Dodge, and Sponge tools on the peeled paint shapes.

16. Using the Magic Wand with a Tolerance of 5, select the area where no peeled paint shapes appear in the C2 layer. Select Inverse, and then save the selection. You may need it later.

17. Make the original Color layer active, and link both the C2 and the C3 layers to it. Select Merge Linked from the layers palette.

18. Use a small Airbrush with the following settings:

Figure 7.27   The peel paint shapes after the Burn, Dodge, and Sponge tools have been applied.

- Pressure: 50%
- Diameter: 3 pixels
- Hardness: 100%
- Spacing: 25%
- Default Angle and Roundness

Create some random marks all over the Color layer using the Eyedropper tool to select a variety of colors from the image (see Figure 7.28).

19. To complete the Color layer for the burn marks, select Filter| Noise|Add Noise. In the dialog box, set the Amount to 8, select Uniform, and check the Monochromatic box.

Now that you've completed the Color layer, you can get to work on the bump map for the burnt look.

Creating A Bump Map For Burn Marks

1. Make a duplicate of the Color layer, and name it "Bump".

2. Select Image|Adjust|Hue/Saturation, and reduce the Saturation to -100.

3. Make a duplicate of the Bump layer, name it "Specularity", and then make it invisible (you'll need it later).

4. Moving back to the Bump layer, select the Lasso tool. Then, make a selection to the far right in the darkened area of the Bump layer, as shown in Figure 7.29.

5. Choose Select|Feather, and feather the selection by 10 pixels.

6. Save the selection.

7. Select Filter|Texture|Texturizer. Then, use these settings:
   - Texture: Sandstone
   - Scaling: 50%

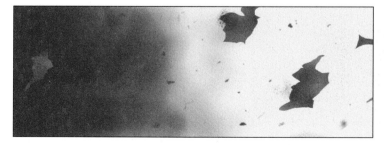

Figure 7.28 The Color layer after applying the random marks.

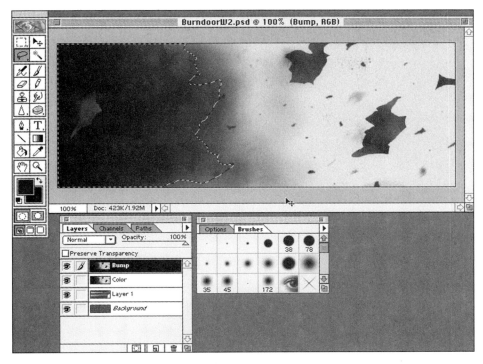

Figure 7.29 The far right selection of the darkened area.

- Relief: 4
- Light Direction: Top Left

Figure 7.30 shows the results.

8. Load the saved selection.

9. Select Image|Adjust|Brightness/Contrast. In the dialog box, set the Brightness to +100 and the Contrast to +53. These settings should make the grays on the left and right sides of the Bump layer pretty equal.

10. Choose Select|Inverse.

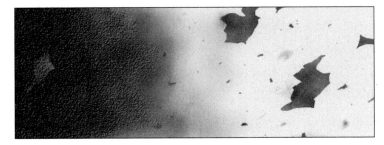

Figure 7.30 The results of the Sandstone filter.

11. Because a dark band still appears where the Brightness didn't reach, lighten the dark band until it matches the rest of the right side by using the Dodge tool with the following settings:

    - Exposure: 50%
    - Diameter: 35 pixels
    - Hardness: 0%
    - Spacing: 25%
    - Default Angle and Roundness

    After you've applied the tone change with the Dodge tool, the Bump layer should look like Figure 7.31.

12. To take care of those extra peel sections of the image, choose Select|Load Selection (the one of the peeled paint).

13. Remove the two parts of the selection on the far left side by holding down the Option key (Mac) or the Ctrl key (Windows) so that the selection matches Figure 7.32.

14. Select Filter|Noise|Add Noise. In the dialog box, set the Amount to 23, select Gaussian, and check the Monochromatic box.

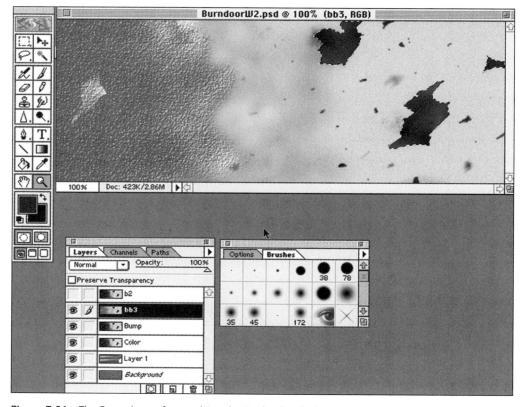

Figure 7.31   The Bump layer after applying the Dodge brush changes.

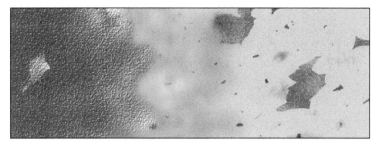

Figure 7.32 The selected areas of the Bump layer.

15. Open the Brightness/Contrast dialog box, and use a Brightness setting of +92 and a Contrast setting of -9. The final Bump layer should look like Figure 7.33.

Now that you've completed your work on the bump layer, you can move on to the specularity map for the burns.

Creating A Specularity Map For Burn Marks

1. Make a duplicate of the Bump layer, and name it "Specularity".

2. Apply Brightness/Contrast to the Specularity layer using a Brightness of -40 and a Contrast of +40.

Finally, you're ready to put together the diffusion map.

Creating A Diffusion Map For Burn Marks

1. Make a duplicate of the Specularity layer, and name it "Diffusion".

2. Apply Brightness/Contrast to the Specularity layer using a Brightness of +17 and a Contrast of -60.

Saving The Image Maps For The Burn Marks

You've completed the Photoshop portion of this burn mark tutorial. Now, you need to save the layers and planar-map them (along the Z axis) onto the 3D object of the door in your 3D program. The resulting image should look something like Figure 7.34.

Now, you can explore one of nature's most troublesome and predominant textures: rust.

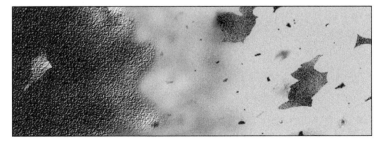

Figure 7.33 The final bump map for the burnt look.

Figure 7.34 The final rendered image of the burnt car door (see figure in Color Studio).

Rust Textures

One of the places where rust is most prevalent is on automobiles. Rust is caused from the combination of age and oxidation. In some of the nation's more frigid areas, rock salt is used to hasten the melting of snow on the roadways. The only trouble with salt on the roads is that it turns cars into rust buckets quicker than you can say "better get Maaco."

Because salt is the number-one candidate in causing rust, you need to visualize how and where rust occurs on an automobile from the presence of road salt. Because salt is laid on the road, rust usually occurs from the bottom up. So, you can now get to work adding some rust to your car door.

Creating A Rust Color Map

1. Open the file called Car door.psd if it is not already open.

2. Create a new layer, and name it "Color".

3. Because salt tends to fade the paint of an automobile, give this car a light yellow color by filling the Color layer with RGB 240, 236, 213.

4. After you paint the car door, create the color for the rust. Most rust comes in a variety of orange hues, so use RGB 207, 133, 67.

5. Double-click on the Paintbrush icon to open its dialog box, and apply the following settings:
   - Opacity: 100%
   - Diameter: 27 pixels
   - Hardness: 0%
   - Spacing: 25%
   - Default Angle and Roundness

6. Paint the orange, rust color from the bottom to the top in semi-circular patterns, as shown in Figure 7.35.

7. Select the Magic Wand tool using a Tolerance of 32 and the Anti-alias box checked.

8. Click on the orange, rust area, and then choose Select|Similar (see Figure 7.36).

9. Choose Select|Save Selection.

10. To add some texture to the rust, select Filter|Noise|Add Noise. In the dialog box, set the Amount to 12, select Gaussian, and check the Monochromatic box.

Figure 7.35 Adding the original rust color.

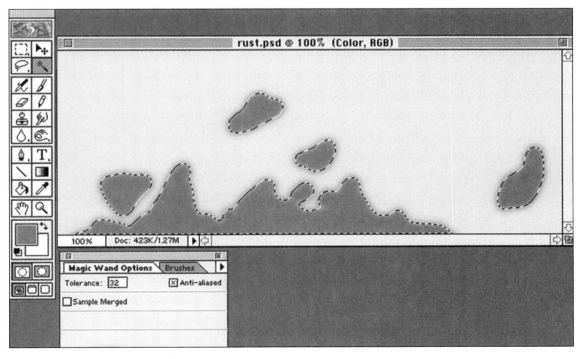

Figure 7.36 Selecting the rust color.

11. Because some color variation usually appears in the areas where the paint meets the rust, you need to do some work on the rust edges. Unless the rust area is already selected, choose Select|Load Selection and load #4.

12. To change the selection to encompass only the edges of the rust, choose Select|Modify|Border. Select a Width of 8 pixels.

13. Select Image|Adjust|Brightness/Contrast. In the dialog box, decrease the Brightness to -76, and leave the Contrast at 0. At this point, the Color layer should look like Figure 7.37.

14. Because the color of the door and rust are still a little too plain, add some variation to it, but first be sure to deselect the border selection by choosing Select|None. To add a little overall variation to the color, select the Burn tool with these settings:

    • Midtones

    • Exposure: 26%

    • Diameter: 65 pixels

    • Hardness: 0%

    • Spacing: 25%

    • Default Angle and Roundness

    Darken the paint and rust surfaces with the Burn tool, as shown in Figure 7.38.

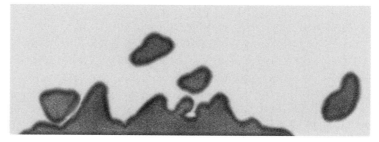

Figure 7.37 The rust area after darkening the border.

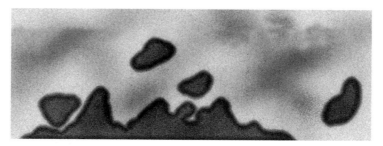

Figure 7.38 The final color map for the rusty car door.

You've completed your work on the color portion of the rusty car door. Now, use the color map to construct the bump, specularity, and diffusion maps.

Creating A Rust Bump Map

1. Make a duplicate of the Color layer, and rename it "Bump".

2. Remove all the color from the Bump layer by selecting Image| Adjust|Hue/Saturation and changing the Saturation to -100.

3. Reload the #4 selection that you saved earlier by choosing Select|Load Selection.

4. To expand the selection to encompass both the rust and edge areas, choose Select|Modify|Expand. Expand by 2 pixels.

5. Select Image|Adjust|Brightness/Contrast. In the dialog box, change the Brightness to +67 and the Contrast to +28. At this point, the Bump layer should resemble Figure 7.39.

6. The paint section of this map still has too much noise, which causes the nonrust areas to look a bit bumpy. To fix this problem, choose Select|Inverse and apply the Filter|Blur|Gaussian Blur command. Use a Gaussian Blur Radius of 2.3 pixels. Now, the "Bump" layer should match Figure 7.40.

You've completed the Bump layer for the rusty car door. Now, use this Bump layer to create the door's specularity map.

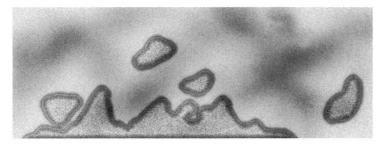

Figure 7.39   The Bump layer after adjusting Brightness/Contrast.

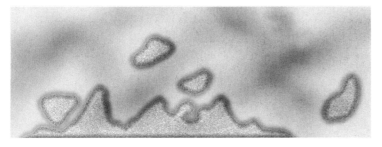

Figure 7.40   The final Bump layer for the rusty car door.

Creating A Rust Specularity Map

1. Duplicate the Bump layer, and rename it "Specularity".

2. Choose Image|Adjust|Invert.

3. Select the Load Selection command again.

4. Choose Select|Inverse.

5. Open the Brightness/Contrast dialog box, and decrease the Brightness to -23 and the Contrast to -94. These settings should give you a specularity map matching Figure 7.41.

Now that you've got your color, bump, and specularity maps in order, you can create the final image map for the rusty car door's diffusion.

Creating A Rust Diffusion Map

1. Make a duplicate of the Bump layer, and rename it "Diffusion".

2. Open the Brightness/Contrast dialog box, and increase the diffusion map's Brightness to +35 and decrease its Contrast to -70 (see Figure 7.42).

Saving The Image Maps

At this point, you've created all the image maps that you need for the rusty car door. And you're ready to save the original Photoshop file with all its layers intact. Copy each of the layers as separate image files that your 3D program can open. Planar-map each of the color, bump,

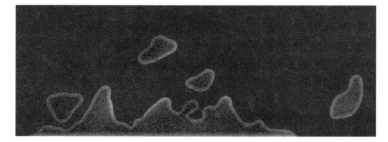

Figure 7.41   The final Specularity layer for the rusty car door.

Figure 7.42   The final diffusion map for the rusty car door.

specularity, and diffusion maps onto the 3D car door, which can be found on the chapt7\Models folder in a variety of formats. To see what the texturizing efforts have produced, take a look at Figure 7.43.

As you can see, the car door looks okay, but it still has a few problems. First, the rust looks a little too shiny. To remedy this situation, all you need to do is darken the rust areas of the specularity map using the Burn tool with the following brush settings:

- Midtones

- Exposure: 50%

- Diameter: 9 pixels

- Hardness: 0%

- Spacing: 25%

- Default Angle and Roundness

Paint out the lighter areas of the rust to take care of the shiny problem. The other problem is that the color for the rust and car body are not dark enough. To fix this problem, all you need to do is open the diffusion map and darken it by using Brightness/Contrast. Change the Brightness to -15 and the Contrast to +10. Now see what the car door looks like after you reapply the specularity and diffusion maps (see Figure 7.44).

Sometimes, you may need to perform several test renders before you're happy with the final results. After all, knowing exactly what your image maps are going to look like before you've applied them to the 3D model is pretty difficult.

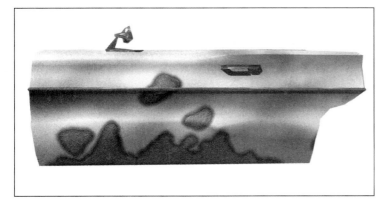

Figure 7.43   The first test render of the rusty car door.

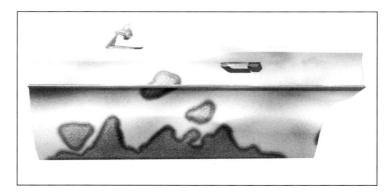

Figure 7.44 The final render of the rusty car door (see figure in Color Studio).

Moving On

Obviously, I simply don't have the space to discuss all the other industrial textures here; however, you can easily modify the techniques
covered in this chapter to create many other types of textures. In the
next chapter, you'll examine some more industrial textures—only they
will be a bit more fantastical in nature. So get ready to create some of
those ever-popular, science fiction textures.

COLOR STUDIO

On the following pages, you'll see color examples of the textures and final renders presented in this book.

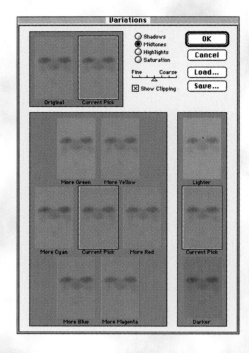

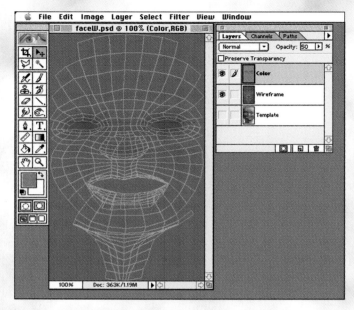

From Chapter 1, the Variations dialog box for the Face.psd image (left) and the same image's Wireframe layer after moving it to beneath the color layer (right).

From Chapter 2, a fractal pattern created by applying the Clouds filter (left), the same pattern using the Difference Clouds filter with a dark green foreground color (center), and a light blue foreground color (right).

From Chapter 2, a leaf pattern before (above) and after (right) aging.

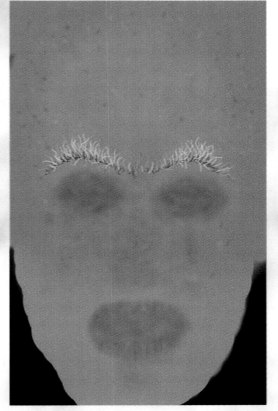

From Chapter 2, the final cracked rock pattern created with a fractal image (above) and the color map for a face without whiskers (right).

From Chapter 3, the hot spots circled on a scanned leaf of ivy (left) and then removed with the Rubber Stamp tool (right).

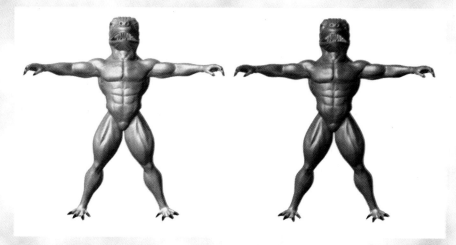

From Chapter 4, the creature on the left is shown without diffusion while the one on the right has a diffusion map applied to it with the diffusion set to 90%.

From Chapter 4, a luminousity map (top), and the luminosity map applied to the side of a spaceship (bottom).

From Chapter 5, a burger and fries in 3D.

From Chapter 5, Sergeant Spore battling the Madagascar beetles.

From Chapter 5, a jungle scene.

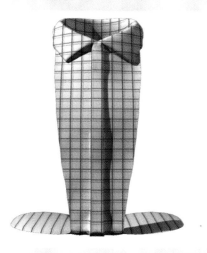

From Chapter 6, a rendered shirt with no texture maps (left) and the final render of the shirt with image maps applied (right).

From Chapter 6, the character Gorg before (left) and after (right) image maps are applied.

From Chapter 7, a dirtless car door (top) and a final rendering of a dirty car door (bottom).

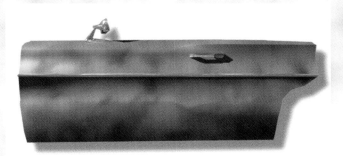

From Chapter 7, the final renders of the car door with chipped paint (top) and layered paint (bottom).

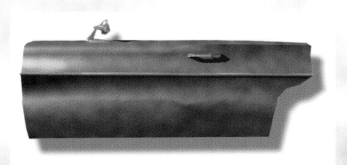

From Chapter 7, the final renders of the burnt car door (top) and the rusty car door (bottom).

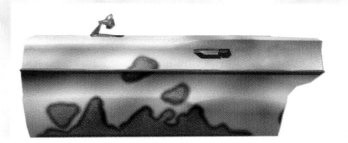

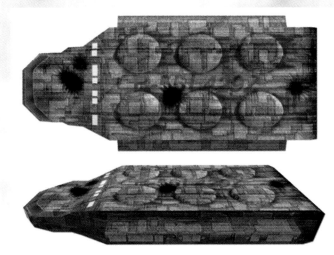

From Chapter 8, the final images of the spaceship (top), molten rock planet (below left), and nebula (below right).

From Chapter 8, the culmination of the three previous images for a photorealistic science fiction scene.

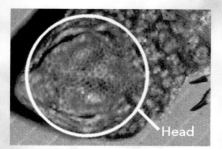

Head

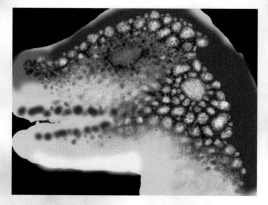

From Chapter 9, the undertone color (above right),
the final color map (right), and the final rendered
image of the side of Gorg's head (above).

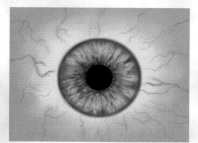

From Chapter 9, the color map of Dr.
Dread's eye (above) and the final render of
Dr. Dread with wrinkles (left).

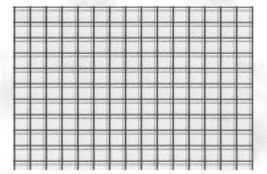

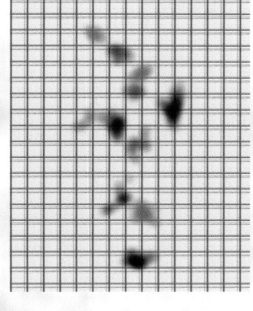

From Chapter 10, the tiled color map for Dr. Dread's shirt (above), the color swatch for the shirt stains (below) and the final render of the shirt (right).

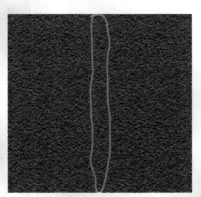

From Chapter 11, images of the dirt image map, including the color layer after adjusting hue and saturation (above left), the tile test with the seam circled in red (above right), and the completed color map (right).

From Chapter 11, the final rendered rock.

The basic rock color.

Adding some purple.

Applying some blue variation.

The completed color map.

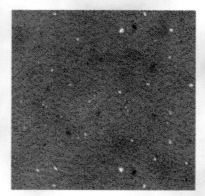

The Color layer after making it seamless.

The final bump map for the rock.

From Chapter 11, the final rendered leaf.

Looking through the Color layer to use the black-and-white leaf image as a guide.

The Color layer after applying the Burn tool.

The final Color layer.

From Chapter 12, the terrain diffusion map after applying the Difference Clouds filter (left) and after removing its color (right).

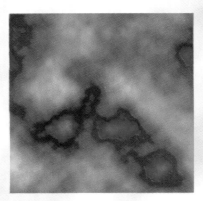

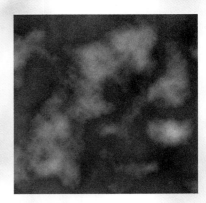

From Chapter 12, the final rendered images of the terrain.

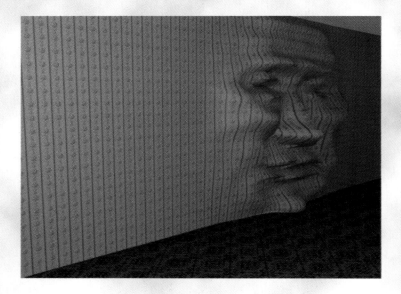

From Chapter 12, the results of using the displacement map applied to a 3D plane (above) and the last frame of the displacement map animation (left).

From Chapter 13, the final rendering of the 3D cow in a field with the light gel applied to a spotlight.

The image after applying the Render Clouds filter.

The image after applying the Paint Daubs filter.

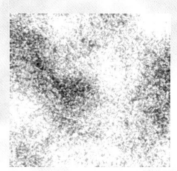

The leaf shadow light gel.

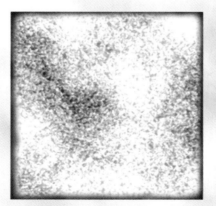

The final leaf shadow light gel.

The rendered scene without the leaf shadow light gel.

From Chapter 13, the final rendering of the room with the psychedelic light gel applied.

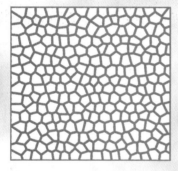

The light gel after applying the Stained Glass filter.

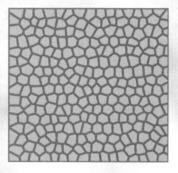

The image after adding the light blue color to the cells.

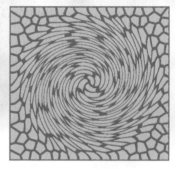

The image after applying the Twirl filter.

The image after applying the Difference Clouds filter.

The scene without the psychedelic light gel.

PAINTING SCIENCE FICTION TEXTURES

8

Science fiction is perhaps more popular today than it ever was, in part because of the breathtaking visual effects created with 3D art and animation. In this chapter, you'll explore just how you can make your 3D science fiction scenes and animations come alive with texture maps.

Whether it be in blockbuster movies such as *Lost in Space* and *Star Wars* or in hit TV shows such as *Babylon 5*, 3D art and animation abound. The realism has become so tangible in these films and shows that the viewer can nearly experience what it would be like to go on a journey through a nebula or to navigate an asteroid field. You can learn how to create your own science fiction effects, such as the ones covered in this chapter:

- Spaceship textures
  - Metal plates
  - Grease and grime
  - Engine exhaust burns
  - Weapon blasts
- Star fields
- Planets
- Nebula

If you want to create a science fiction scene, you need some way of getting the viewer into outer space. You can get started now by creating some spaceship textures.

Creating Spaceship Textures

Before you start creating the textures for your spaceship, or even before you begin modeling it, you need to consider several questions. First, where is this spaceship coming from? Is it an alien ship? Was it created on earth? If so, in what year was it created? What is the spaceship made of? Is it constructed from some futuristic alloy not yet invented, or is it made of some familiar metal? Has it seen battle? Was it built as a passenger, war, or cargo vessel? How many people or aliens is it built to hold? Finally, what is its history? The more questions you ask about the spaceship, the more realistic it will become in your mind, and the more realistic it becomes in your mind, the more realism you'll be able to convey to the viewer.

Take a look at the raw material for the 3D spaceship you'll be working with in Figure 8.1.

This spaceship doesn't really look like much, does it? That's why texture mapping is so important. Three-dimensional models in their raw, nontextured form generally lack any kind of realism. I can assure you, however, by the time you're finished texturing this ship, it'll be ready to explore infinity and beyond. For now, take a look at the ship's history.

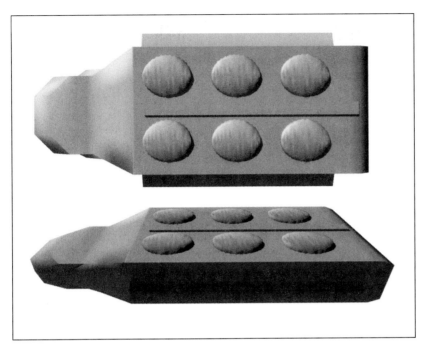

Figure 8.1 The spaceship model with no textures applied to it.

The Spaceship's History

This particular ship began as a B-class cargo freighter in the year 2041. Its main purpose was to transport minerals from the asteroid belt to the processing plants on the moon. The vessel's captain, William Forrester, was markedly one of the best solo captains of the B-class fleet. But Forrester gradually became disillusioned with the ever-constricting insurance laws, bureaucracy, and the underhanded larceny of the galactic corporations. One day, Forrester caved in under the weight of hypocrisy and stole the B-class freighter to make his living as a black-market goods runner. He took the ship to an off-world colony where a friend revamped the engines, added guns, and basically changed it from a cargo vessel into a state-of-the-art renegade space craft capable of light speed and tactical maneuvers if necessary. Forrester and, more important, the former freighter are covetously sought by the World Bank Corporate Government. According to the WBCG's bean counters, it is impossible that a B-class freighter, no matter how much it was modified, could evade the authorities for so long on the spatial highways. Forrester has come very close to being caught several times, sustaining considerable damage to his ship, but he has always managed to break free.

Armed with this much history for your spaceship, you're ready to build and surface it. Now, you can see quite clearly in your mind's eye just what the ship might look like. Because you know that the ship was a cargo freighter, it had to be built tough. This ship would definitely be made of some rugged material such as metal.

Adding Metal Plates To The Spaceship

Now, you can get to work covering the ship with tough metal plates by following these steps:

1. Open the file called Shiptop.psd from the chapt8\Spaceship folder on the CD-ROM.

2. Open the Layers palette for the file either by selecting Window|Show Layers or by pressing the F7 key on your keyboard. You should see two layers here already. The bottommost layer, named Wire, contains the wireframe of the top view of the spaceship. The second layer, called Template, contains a rendered view of the spaceship.

3. Create a new layer, and name it "Color".

4. Create a new, darker tan color as the foreground color, RGB 138, 123, 109.

5. Choose Edit|Fill. Choose Foreground, set Opacity to 100%, and set the Mode to Normal.

6. Select Filter|Stylize|Tiles. Set the Number of Tiles to 7 and Maximum Offset to 60%.

7. Reapply this filter with the exact same settings once again (see Figure 8.2).

8. Click on the foreground color, and change it to a dark brown, RGB 43, 38, 34.

9. Double-click on the Magic Wand tool, and set the Tolerance to 1 pixel. Then, make sure that the Anti-Aliased button is unchecked.

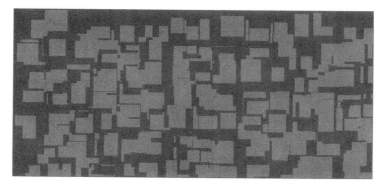

Figure 8.2 The Color layer after applying the Tiles filter twice.

10. Using the Magic Wand tool, click on the light tan area of the image.

11. Choose Select|Select Similar.

12. Select Edit|Stroke, and apply the following settings:
    - Stroke Width: 1 pixel
    - Location: Inside
    - Opacity: 100%
    - Mode: Normal

    After you apply the stroke, the image should look like Figure 8.3.

13. From the Layers palette, select Duplicate Layer and rename this new layer "Bump".

14. Make this layer invisible by clicking on the eye to the far left of the Bump layer.

15. Make the Color layer active by clicking on it.

16. Select Filter|Texture|Grain. Under the Options, set the Intensity to 45, the Contrast to 5, and the Grain Type to Horizontal. The effect should look like Figure 8.4.

Seeing that you're working with a B-class cargo freighter, some identification markings are in order.

Adding Identification Markings To The Spaceship

1. Set the Opacity of the Color layer to 55%. This setting allows you to see the Template layer, which lies directly beneath it.

2. Click on the foreground color, and change it to an off-red, RGB 190, 50, 50.

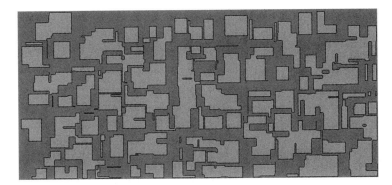

Figure 8.3   The image after applying the Stroke command.

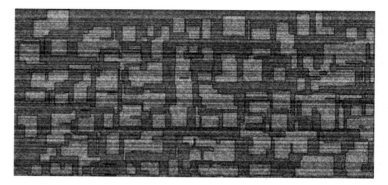

Figure 8.4 The Color layer after applying the Grain filter.

3. Select the Text tool from the toolbox. Click on the area that lies between the two series of disks on the top of the ship to open the dialog box. In the text section, type "B-55L429Z". Set the Font to Helvetica Bold, set the Size to 50 points, and be sure to check the Auto kern and Anti-alias radio buttons.

4. After you get the text situated exactly where you want it, select Layer|Type|Render Layer. The Color layer should now look something like Figure 8.5.

5. Double-click on the Burn tool, and set the Burn Options to Midtones and the Exposure to 52%. Apply the following brush settings:

   • Diameter: 9 pixels

   • Hardness: 0%

   • Spacing: 25%

   • Default Angle and Roundness

6. Burn some of the edges of the letters, as shown in Figure 8.6.

7. Link the Color layer with the Letters layer that you just created, and select Merge Linked from the Layers palette.

Figure 8.5 The color map after adding the text.

Figure 8.6   The Color layer after applying the Burn tool to some of the letters.

Because this spaceship is to be piloted by a human being—Captain Forrester—providing him with some means of viewing outer space from within the ship's cockpit is a good idea. For this purpose, you need to create a windshield.

Creating A Spaceship Windshield

1. Create a new bluish gray as the foreground color, RGB 84, 89, 118.

2. Select the Polygonal Lasso tool by clicking on it or by pressing the L key on your keyboard.

3. Set the Opacity of the Color layer to 14%.

4. Using the Polygonal Lasso tool, create a windshield, as shown in Figure 8.7.

5. Select Edit|Fill. Then, choose Foreground Color, set the Opacity to 100%, and leave the Mode set to Normal.

6. Choose Select|Save Selection, and name your selection "Windshield". You'll need this selection later. The Color layer should look like Figure 8.8 at this point.

Figure 8.7   The selection for the windshield of the spaceship.

Figure 8.8 The Color map after creating the windshield's color.

7. One problem with this windshield is that the color is a little too bland. You can fix this problem by double-clicking on the Burn tool and setting it to Midtones and setting the Exposure to 52%. Then, apply the following brush settings:

   - Diameter: 9 pixels
   - Hardness: 0%
   - Spacing: 25%
   - Default Angle and Roundness

8. Use the Burn tool to add some variation to the windshield of the spaceship, as shown in Figure 8.9.

Using the same settings for the Burn tool, create some streaks across the back of the spaceship, as shown in Figure 8.10.

Now that you've completed the rudimentary work for the color image map, you still need to add the bump, specularity, diffusion, and luminosity maps to the spaceship.

Figure 8.9 The color map of the spaceship after adding some variation to the windshield by using the Burn tool.

Figure 8.10 The spaceship color map after applying some streaks with the Burn tool.

Creating The Bump Map For The Spaceship

1. Click on the Bump layer that you created earlier to make it active.

2. Choose Select|Load Selection. From the Channels menu, select Windshield.

3. Select the Magic Wand tool, and click on the darker brown area of the Bump layer, RGB 138, 123, 109.

4. Select Edit|Fill. Then, choose Foreground Color, set Opacity to 100%, and leave the Mode set to Normal.

5. Change the foreground color to black, RGB 0, 0, 0.

6. Choose Edit|Stroke. Set the Width to 1 pixel, the Location to Inside, and the Opacity to 100%. The Bump layer should match Figure 8.11 at this point.

7. Because you're working with a bump map, color is unnecessary. Remove the color by selecting Image|Adjust|Hue/Saturation. Change the Saturation to -100, and leave the other sliders alone.

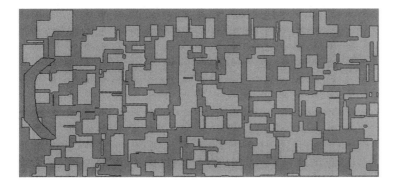

Figure 8.11 The Bump layer after applying the stroke to the windshield.

8. The Bump layer could use a little more detail. Select Filter|Brush Strokes|Ink Outlines. Set the Stroke Length to 27, the Dark Intensity to 16, and the Light Intensity to 3. The results should match those shown in Figure 8.12.

9. The Windshield would look better if it were recessed a bit. To recess the windshield of the ship, choose Select|Load Selection. From the Channels menu, select Windshield.

10. Change the foreground color to a dark gray, RGB 39, 39, 39.

11. Select Edit|Fill. Then, choose Foreground Color, set Opacity to 100%, and leave the Mode set to Normal.

12. Drop the selection by choosing Select|Deselect or by pressing Command+D (Mac) or Alt+D (Windows). The image should look like Figure 8.13 at this point.

The details for the spaceship are pretty good right now, but often filters alone don't give you the control over the exact look that you want. Sometimes, you actually need to use the painting tools to create the details that you want.

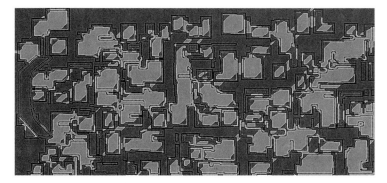

Figure 8.12 The Bump layer after applying the Ink Outlines filter.

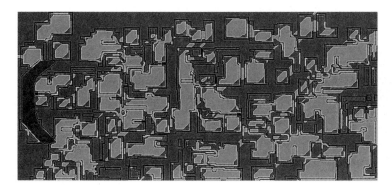

Figure 8.13 The Bump layer after darkening the windshield.

Creating Details On The Spaceship With The Painting Tools

1. Change the foreground color to white, RGB 255, 255, 255.

2. Double-click on the Paintbrush icon to open its options dialog box.

3. Set the brush to Normal and the Opacity to 100%. Create a brush with the following settings:
   - Diameter: 16 pixels
   - Hardness: 100%
   - Spacing: 25%
   - Default Angle and Roundness

4. Make the Bump layer semitransparent by setting the layer's Opacity to 48%.

5. Create some circles in the light areas of the spaceship's bump map by doing single mouse clicks with the Paintbrush, as shown in Figure 8.14. When the bump map is applied to the surface of the 3D spaceship, these circles will appear as elevated disks when the ship is rendered.

6. To add some additional details, such as some rectangular elevations, you need to load the square brushes into the brush panel. To do so, double-click on the Paintbrush icon to open the Paintbrush Options dialog box.

7. Click on the Brushes tab.

8. In the upper-right corner of the Brushes palette, select Load Brushes.

9. Locate your Photoshop folder. In the Goodies folder, locate and open the Brushes folder; then open the Square Brushes. The Square Brushes will then automatically load into your Brushes palette.

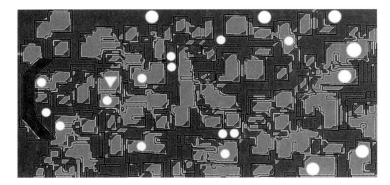

Figure 8.14 The bump map after adding some circles with the paintbrush.

10. Select the square brush shown in Figure 8.15.

11. Use this brush with the white paint to create rectangular elevations on the ship, as shown in Figure 8.16.

You've now completed the work you need to do on the bump map for this particular section. Next, you can create the specularity map for the spaceship.

Creating The Spaceship's Specularity Map

1. Make the Bump layer active by clicking on it.

2. Select Duplicate layer from the Layers palette.

3. Name this new layer "Specularity".

4. Select Image|Adjust|Invert.

5. Select Image|Adjust|Brightness/Contrast. In the dialog box, set the Brightness to -100 and the Contrast to -97.

6. Select Image|Adjust|Brightness/Contrast once again, and set the Brightness to -33 and the Contrast to -43.

7. Choose Select|Load Selection. Then, choose Windshield from the Channels menu once again.

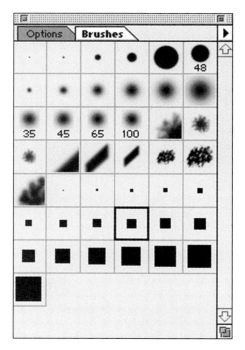

Figure 8.15 Selecting the square brush.

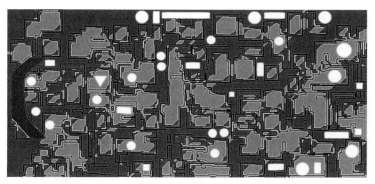

Figure 8.16 The bump map for the spaceship after adding the rectangular elevations with the square paintbrush.

8. With the Windshield area selected, select Image|Adjust|Brightness/ Contrast. In the dialog box, increase the Brightness to +37, and leave the Contrast set to 0.

9. Because this particular ship has seen some pretty rough celestial action, you should rough up its surface a little. To do so, select Filter|Add Noise. Set the Amount to 3, set the Distribution to Uniform, and make sure to check the Monochromatic radio button.

Now that you've completed the work you need to do for the ship's specularity map, you can move on to creating the diffusion map.

Creating The Spaceship's Diffusion Map

1. Make the Color layer active by clicking on it.

2. Select Duplicate layer from the Layers palette.

3. Name this new layer "Diffusion".

4. Make the Diffusion layer black and white by selecting Image| Adjust|Hue/Saturation. Slide the Saturation slider all the way to the left to -100, and leave the other sliders alone. The diffusion map should look like Figure 8.17 at this stage.

5. The image is still a little too harsh to be used as a diffusion map. You can fix this problem by selecting Image|Adjust|Brightness/ Contrast, and in the dialog box , setting the Brightness to +78 and the Contrast to -76. The diffusion map should now look like Figure 8.18.

That exercise completes the work needed for the diffusion map. Now, you can add some running lights to the spacecraft by creating a luminosity map.

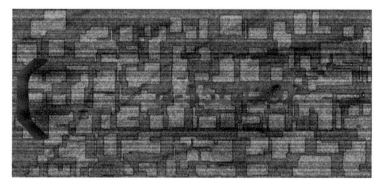

Figure 8.17 After removing all the color from the diffusion map.

Figure 8.18 The diffusion map after adjusting its brightness and contrast.

Creating The Luminosity Map For The Spaceship

1. To begin, you need to create the color for the lights that will be added to your original color map layer. Create a new layer, and name it "Color2".

2. Change the foreground color to a red, RGB 204, 3, 3.

3. Double-click on the Paintbrush icon. Set the Paintbrush Options to Normal and the Opacity to 100%. Give the brush the following settings:

   - Diameter: 16 pixels
   - Hardness: 100%
   - Spacing: 25%
   - Default Angle and Roundness

4. Using single mouse clicks, place red lights in the areas shown in Figure 8.19.

5. Now that the running lights are in place, you need to add some windows. After all, you don't want the pilot to become claustrophobic way out there in the cosmos. To ensure that the windows line up accurately, you can use Photoshop's guides. To do so, select View|Rulers.

6. Drag the mouse from the far left ruler to just behind the spaceship's windshield, as shown in Figure 8.20.

7. Double-click on the Paintbrush icon to open its palette.

8. Select the square brush shown in Figure 8.21.

9. Change the foreground color to a light yellow, RGB 254, 243, 197.

10. Using the square paintbrush, create a series of windows along the vertical guide, as shown in Figure 8.22.

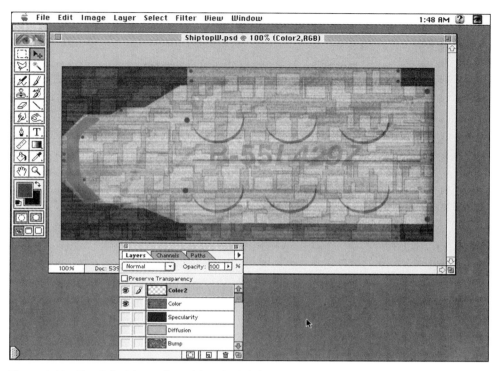

Figure 8.19 The Color2 layer after adding the lights.

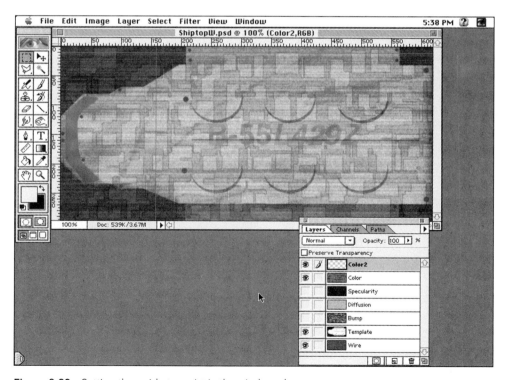

Figure 8.20 Setting the guide to assist in the window placement.

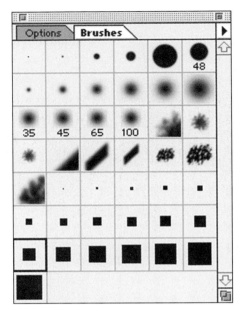

Figure 8.21 The square paintbrush used to create the spaceship's windows.

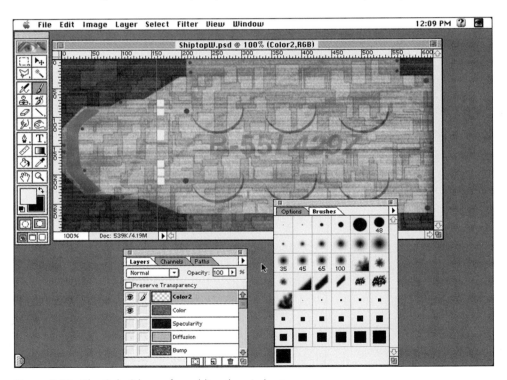

Figure 8.22 The Color2 layer after adding the windows.

11. To add some luminosity to the windshield, choose Select|Load Selection. From the Channels menu, select Windshield.

12. Using the light yellow color that you used for the other windows (RGB 254, 243, 197) select Edit|Fill. Then, choose Foreground Color, set Opacity to 100%, and leave the Mode set to Normal.

13. You still need to add the colors of the Color2 layer to the Color layer. Make a duplicate of the Color2 layer by selecting Duplicate Layer from the Layers palette, and rename this new layer "Luminosity".

14. Make the Color2 layer active by clicking on it.

15. Choose Select|Load Selection. Then, choose Windshield from the Channels menu.

16. Press the Delete key on your keyboard to erase the light yellow color from the layer.

17. Make the Color layer active by clicking on it. Link the Color layer to the Color2 layer, and then select Merge Linked from the Layers palette.

18. Make the Color2 copy layer active by clicking on it.

19. Double-click on the Color2 copy layer's name, and rename it "Luminosity".

20. From the Layers palette, select New Layer.

21. Press the D key on your keyboard to get black in the foreground color layer.

22. Choose Select|All.

23. Select Edit|Fill. Then, choose Foreground Color, set Opacity to 100%, and leave the Mode set to Normal. Fill this new layer with the black color.

24. Move the new layer so that it lies directly beneath the Luminosity layer, as shown in Figure 8.23.

25. Click on the Luminosity layer to make it active.

26. Link the black layer to the Luminosity layer.

27. Select Merge|Linked from the Layers palette.

Now you've completed your work on the Luminosity layer. I know, this project took quite a few steps, but your work will pay off once you've mapped each of these image maps onto the 3D model and rendered it.

Select each of the Color, Bump, Specularity, Diffusion, and Luminosity layers individually, and save each one as a separate image file in a format that your 3D program can read. Map each of them onto the 3D model of the spaceship that I've provided for you in a variety of 3D formats on the CD-ROM. You can find the Spaceship file under the chapt8models\SpaceshipModels folder.

After you load the image maps into your 3D program, planar-map them onto the top of the spaceship along the Y (up and down) axis. When the image is rendered, it should look like Figure 8.24.

As you know, this B-class cargo freighter, piloted and stolen by Captain Forrester, has seen quite a few venturesome battles through the years. Obviously, the spaceship would have quite a few battle scars, so now you can get to work adding weapon blast scars to the ship.

To create these scars, you can create a paintbrush that facilitates the process. To create a weapon blast paintbrush, you just need to follow a few simple steps.

Figure 8.23 The image after moving the black layer so that it lies directly beneath the Luminosity layer.

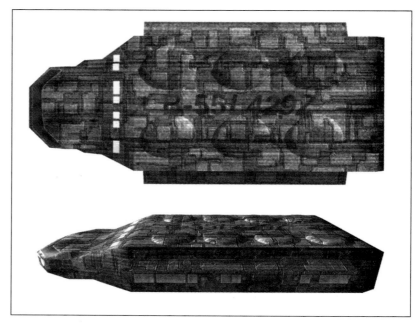

Figure 8.24 The rendered spaceship.

Creating A Weapon Blast Brush

1. Double-click on the Airbrush icon. Set the Airbrush Options to Normal and the Pressure to 100%. Give the brush the following settings:

   - Diameter: 9 pixels
   - Hardness: 0%
   - Spacing: 25%
   - Default Angle and Roundness

2. Press the D key to put black, RGB 0, 0, 0 in the foreground layer.

3. Select File|New, and set the Contents to White and the size to 100×100 pixels.

Note: *In the rendered image (Figure 8.24), I've taken the liberty to surface the sides, front, and back of the spaceship. The image maps for these surfaces came from copying portions of the image maps that you just created.*

4. Use the Airbrush to create a small black splotch on the white background, as shown in Figure 8.25.

5. Double-click on the Smudge tool icon to open the Smudge Options. Set the Pressure to 67%. Create a brush with the following settings:

   - Diameter: 5 pixels
   - Hardness: 0%
   - Spacing: 25%
   - Default Angle and Roundness

6. Using the Smudge tool, pull from the center of the black color toward the outer edges of the white, as shown in Figure 8.26.

7. Continue pulling the black from the central black splotch until the weapon blast looks like Figure 8.27.

8. Select the Cropping tool, and crop the blast image so that it matches Figure 8.28.

9. Choose Select|All.

10. From the Brush Options palette, select the pull-down menu from the upper-right corner, and select Define Brush. You've now created a weapon blast brush and should be able see the brush as a selectable item in the palette.

11. Open the Shiptop.psd file that you used earlier.

12. Click on the Color layer to make it active.

13. Make sure that black (RGB 0, 0, 0) is still in the foreground Color layer.

14. Change the Color layer's Opacity to 67%, and arrange the layers so that you can see the Wireframe layer through the Color layer.

15. Using the weapon blast brush, create several blast marks on the Color layer, as shown in Figure 8.29.

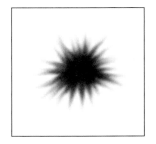

Figure 8.28 The blast image after cropping it.

Figure 8.25 The beginning of the blast scar.

Figure 8.26 The beginning of the weapon blast brush.

Figure 8.27 The weapon blast after applying the Smudge tool.

Figure 8.29 The Color layer after adding the blast marks.

Because you've created some great weapon blasts for the Color layer, accentuating the color map by adding the weapon blast marks to the bump map is a good idea.

Adding The Weapon Blast Marks To The Bump Map

1. Leave the Color layer with an Opacity setting of 67% so that you can see through it.

2. Make the Bump layer active by clicking on it.

3. Using the weapon blast brush that you just created, match up the brush to the place where the blast marks appear on the Color layer. After you line up the blast marks, the Bump layer should look like Figure 8.30.

Save the Color and Bump layers in a format that your 3D program can read. Map these layers onto the 3D spaceship that I've provided in the chapt8models\SpaceshipModels folder on the CD-ROM. You will find several 3D formats in this folder. Just open one that your 3D program can read. Planar-map the new color and bump maps along the

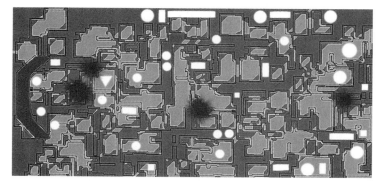

Figure 8.30 The Bump layer after applying the blast marks with the weapons blast brush.

Y axis onto the top of the spaceship. Use the specularity, diffusion, and luminosity maps that you created earlier in the chapter to map the ship for those specific channels. The final, rendered spaceship should look like Figure 8.31.

Now that you've added the blast marks to the spaceship, you need to create some burn marks where the ship's jets are.

Creating Engine Exhaust Burns

When metal becomes heated, especially at very high temperatures, the carbon in the metal turns black. To create this effect, you just need to follow a few steps:

1. Open the Layers palette, and click on the Color layer to make it active.

2. Double-click on the Burn tool icon. Change its settings to Midtones, and set the Exposure to 78%. Use a brush with the following settings:

   - Diameter: 35 pixels
   - Hardness: 0%
   - Spacing: 25%
   - Default Angle and Roundness

3. Darken the rear (the far right) of the spaceship Color layer, as shown in Figure 8.32.

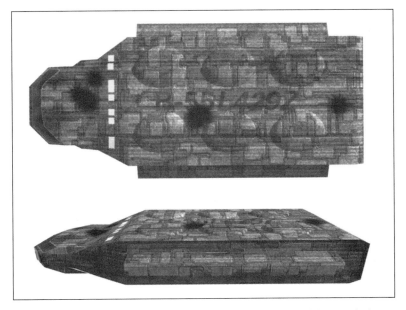

Figure 8.31   The rendered image of the spaceship after the blast marks have been added.

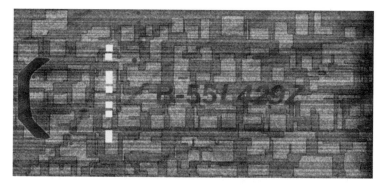

Figure 8.32 The Color layer after applying the Burn tool to the rear of the ship.

4. Click on the Diffusion layer to make it active.

5. Using the Burn tool with the same settings as shown in Step 2, darken the back portion of the ship's Diffusion layer. To see what the Diffusion layer should look like after applying this operation, take a look at Figure 8.33.

Now that the spaceship has its metal plates, blast marks, and burn marks, the final operation is to add some grease stains to the surface of the spaceship.

Adding Grease Stains To The Spaceship

Through the years, Captain Forrester has transported some pretty nasty cargo in his B-class cargo freighter. This material has left stains behind on the surface of the ship. To create these stains, follow these steps:

1. Make the Color layer active by clicking on it.

2. Change the Color layer's Opacity to 48% so that you can see the Wireframe layer through it.

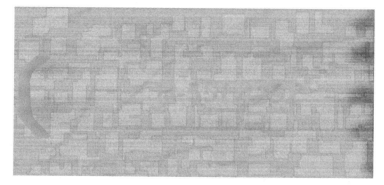

Figure 8.33 The diffusion map after applying the Burn tool to the rear of the ship.

3. Click on the foreground Color layer, and change it to a dark blue oil color, RGB 32, 34, 52.

4. Make the Color layer invisible by clicking on the eye icon in the Layers palette. Make the Wireframe layer active by clicking on it.

5. Choose the Elliptical selection tool from the toolbar.

6. Using the Wire layer as a reference, select each of the circular disks, as shown in Figure 8.34.

7. Create the effect that grease (or some other viscous liquid) has escaped from these cylinders and marred the spaceship's surface. To make the grease painting process easier, choose Select|Inverse. Now the disks are masked; they will not receive any of the color changes that you apply.

8. Double-click on the Airbrush tool to open its options dialog box.

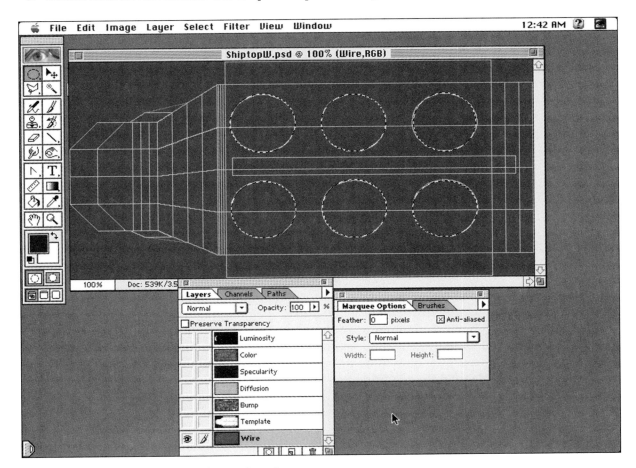

Figure 8.34   The disks selected from the Wireframe layer.

9. Set the Airbrush Options to Normal with a Pressure setting of 30%. For the brush, use the following settings:

- Diameter: 9 pixels
- Hardness: 0%
- Spacing: 25%
- Default Angle and Roundness

10. Create the oil leaks around the disks, as shown in Figure 8.35.

You've now completed the work on the spaceship. You just need to save the new Color layer in a format that your 3D program can read and planar-map the image along the Y axis onto the top of the spaceship. Take a look at Figure 8.36 to see what the completed spaceship looks like after it's rendered with the metal plates, blast marks, burn marks, and grease stain effects.

Another integral part of any science fiction scene are the stars that fill the background. Fortunately, creating starfields is pretty simple with Photoshop.

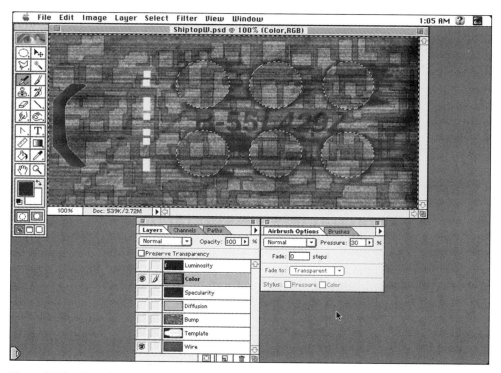

Figure 8.35 The color map after applying the grease stains.

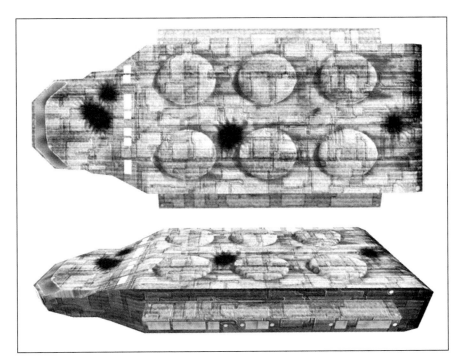

Figure 8.36 The completed spaceship rendered (see figure in Color Studio).

Creating Star Fields

Creating a seamless, tileable map for the star field is a good idea. Star fields usually cover a large area in the 3D scene. With a seamless, tileable star field map, you can simply tile/repeat the stars to cover a large area of space. To get started, just follow these steps:

1. Create a new file that is 500×500 pixels and has a black background.

2. Click on the foreground color, and change it to white, RGB 255, 255, 255.

3. Double-click on the Airbrush icon to open its options dialog box. Select a brush, and set the Options to Normal and the Pressure to 30%. For the brush, use the following settings:

   - Diameter: 9 pixels
   - Hardness: 0%
   - Spacing: 25%
   - Default Angle and Roundness

4. Use this brush to create several blotches in the lower-left corner.

5. Change the brush size diameter to 5 pixels and then to 2 pixels to create several smaller stars in the same lower-left corner, as shown in Figure 8.37.

6. If you look into the sky on a clear night, you'll notice that not all the stars appear as white dots. Some seem to change their color from white to red to blue to orange. These stars may actually be star clusters or distant suns. To emulate this effect and add some variety to your star field, click on the foreground color, and change it to a dark red, RGB 136, 0, 0. Use the Airbrush with the 2-pixel diameter that you used before to add the small white stars.

7. Click on the foreground color, and change it to a dark blue RGB 0, 9, 134. Use the Airbrush with the 2-pixel diameter and the one with the 5-pixel diameter to create some blue stars in the same lower-left corner of the image, as shown in Figure 8.38. (I've also added a few more white stars to fill out this bottom corner of the star field image.)

8. Double-click on the Rubber Stamp icon to open its palette. Set the Rubber Stamp Options to Normal with the Opacity set to 100%. Make sure that the Use All Layers and Aligned boxes are left unchecked.

9. Select a brush for the Rubber Stamp tool with the following settings:
   - Diameter: 48 pixels
   - Hardness: 100%
   - Spacing: 25%
   - Default Angle and Roundness

10. Move the brush over to the lower-left corner. Hold down the Option key (Mac) or Alt key (Windows) to sample some of the stars in that area.

Figure 8.37   The lower-left corner of the star field image after adding a few white stars.

Figure 8.38 The completed lower-left corner of the star field image.

11. Use the Rubber Stamp tool to create stars covering the entire area of the star field image. Be sure to resample different areas where the stars occur so that you can avoid creating stars that noticeably repeat. Take a look at Figure 8.39 to see what the final star field should look like when you're finished.

12. Because you want to make this image to be both seamless and tileable, test the image to see whether any seams appear when you tile it. To do so, choose Select|All.

13. Choose Edit|Define Pattern.

14. Create a new file by choosing File|New, and select a size that is 1,000×1,000 pixels.

15. Select Edit|Fill. Under Contents, set the Options to 100%. Under Blending, leave the Options set to 100% and the Mode set to Normal.

    After the image is filled with the tiled star field, you'll notice that some of the stars in the center and middle areas have been cut off. These cut-off stars have been circled in Figure 8.40.

16. To remove these chopped-off stars, you just need to refer back to the original star field that you created (the nontiled one), and change the foreground color to black, RGB 0, 0, 0.

Figure 8.39 The star field map after filling the entire image with stars using the Rubber Stamp tool.

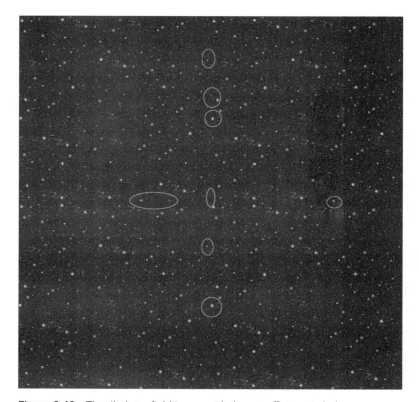

Figure 8.40 The tiled star field image with the cut-off stars circled.

17. Double-click on the Paintbrush icon. Set the Options to Normal with an Opacity setting of 100%. For the brush, use the following settings:
    - Diameter: 5 pixels
    - Hardness: 100%
    - Spacing: 25%
    - Default Angle and Roundness

18. Use the brush to paint out any of the stars that lie directly on or near the outer edges of the star field image. Figure 8.41 shows what the final seamless, tileable star field should look like.

Other elements that will greatly enhance the realism of your science fiction scenes are realistic-looking planets.

> **Note:** Be sure to save the star field file, the planet, and all the spaceship files with their layers intact as Photoshop files just in case you need to refer back them.

Adding Realistic Planets

Most planets in the universe are spherical—at least all the planets that I've seen pictures of. Knowing that you'll be working with a spherical 3D object, you'll obviously want to map the object using the spherical mapping method. To ensure that your image map for the planet will not stretch over the surface of the 3D sphere, you should never use a square image map. You should use an image map that is two and a

Figure 8.41 The completed seamless, tileable star field image.

half times longer than its length from top to bottom. If you have an image map that is 300 pixels from top to bottom, for example, you would want the image map's length to be 750 pixels from left to right. This way, the image map will not stretch.

What Kind Of Planet Do You Want?

A pretty important consideration before beginning to paint the planet map is what type of planet you're going to create? Do you want the surface to be made up of water and earth with an atmosphere and clouds like our planet? Is it going to be composed of gases like Saturn? Or is it going to be dry and rocky like the surface of the moon? After you decide the type of planet you want to add, you can begin the process of constructing your own 3D planet or planets.

Here, you're going to create a planet that is a giant ball of molten lava—much like the earth was millions of years ago.

Creating The Color Image Map For The Molten Planet

1. Create a new file that is 750×300 pixels.

2. Click on the foreground color, and change it to a reddish orange, RGB 255, 92, 20.

3. Select Edit|Fill. Then, choose Foreground Color, set Opacity to 100%, and leave the Mode set to Normal.

4. Choose Filter|Noise|Add Noise. Set the Amount to 64, set the Distribution to Uniform, and leave the Monochromatic radio button unchecked. The results should look like Figure 8.42.

5. Select Filter|Sketch|Plaster, which gives you an image like the one shown in Figure 8.43.

Figure 8.42   The planet Color layer after applying the Noise filter.

Figure 8.43 The image after applying the Plaster filter.

6. Because the Plaster filter removed the color from the image, you can get some of that orange color back by selecting Filter|Fade Plaster. Set the Opacity to 70% and the Mode to Multiply.

7. Select Image|Adjust|Brightness/Contrast. In the dialog box, leave the Brightness set to 0, but increase the Contrast to +21. The planet's color map should look like Figure 8.44.

8. Select Filter|Distort|Ocean Ripple. In the Options dialog box, set the Ripple Size to 4 and the Ripple Magnitude to 8.

9. Select Filter|Fade Ocean Ripple. Fade the Opacity to 45%, and leave the Mode set to Normal. The color map should be similar to Figure 8.45 at this point.

10. Change the foreground color to a bright yellow, RGB 255, 249, 77.

11. Double-click on the Airbrush icon to open its palette. Change the Airbrush Options to Overlay with a Pressure of 30%. Change the brush to the following settings:

    - Diameter: 45 pixels
    - Hardness: 0%
    - Spacing: 25%

Figure 8.44 The color map after applying the Fade filter settings.

Figure 8.45 The color map after applying and then fading the Ocean Ripple effect.

- Default Angle and Roundness

The results of the painting operation should look something like Figure 8.46.

12. Change the foreground color to black, RGB 0, 0, 0.

13. Double-click on the Airbrush icon to open its dialog box. Change the Airbrush Options to Overlay with a Pressure of 30%. Change the brush to the following settings:

   - Diameter: 9 pixels
   - Hardness: 0%
   - Spacing: 25%
   - Default Angle and Roundness

14. Create several dark areas on the image map, as shown in Figure 8.47.

15. The planet's color map looks a little too sharp in certain areas. To fix this problem, select Filter|Blur|Gaussian Blur, and set Radius to 0.9 pixels. The completed color map should look like Figure 8.48.

Now that you've created a great color map for the planet, you still need to need to create a bump map and a diffusion map.

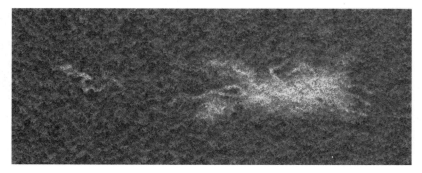

Figure 8.46 The Color layer after adding the yellow.

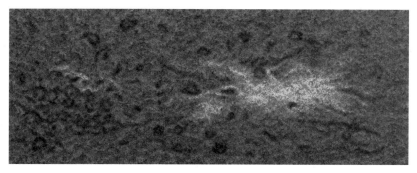

Figure 8.47 The Color layer for the planet after adding dark areas.

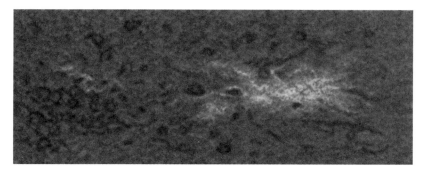

Figure 8.48 The final color map for the molten lava planet.

Creating The Bump Map For The Planet

1. Make sure that the Color layer is active (it must be because it's the only layer present). From the Layers palette, choose Duplicate Layer. Rename this new layer "Bump".

2. Select Image|Adjust|Hue/Saturation, reduce the Saturation to -100, and leave the other sliders alone (left at 0).

That's it for the work on the Bump layer. The completed bump map should look like Figure 8.49.

Next, you need to create the diffusion map for the planet.

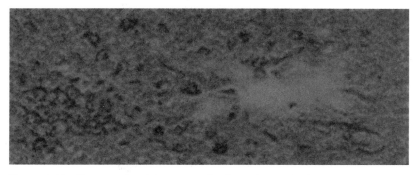

Figure 8.49 The completed bump map for the molten rock planet.

Creating The Diffusion Map For The Molten Rock Planet

1. Make sure that the Bump layer is active by clicking on it.

2. From the Layers palette, select Duplicate layer, and name this new layer "Diffusion".

3. Select Image|Adjust|Brightness/Contrast. In the dialog box set Brightness to +95 and the Contrast to -31. The diffusion map image should look like Figure 8.50.

Now, you've completed all the work you need to create a molten rock planet. Save each of the Color, Bump, and Diffusion layers as separate images in file formats that your 3D program can read. Spherical-map each of these images onto a 3D sphere. Figure 8.51 shows the results of the rendered image.

For the final step in this science fiction space odyssey, you'll learn how to create a nebula.

Figure 8.50   The completed diffusion map for the molten rock planet.

Figure 8.51   The final rendered image of the molten rock planet (see figure in Color Studio).

Stirring Up A Nebula

Nebulae occur in space as interstellar clouds of gas and dust that appear as multicolored mists. These nebulae can span light years of space. Creating an interstellar nebula with Photoshop is a fairly straightforward process; just follow these steps:

1. Open the Photoshop file you created earlier in this chapter for the star field. If you forgot to save the star field file, I've provided it on the CD-ROM. It's called Starfield.psd and can be found in the chapt8\Starfield folder.

2. Create a new layer, and name it "Nebula". In fact, save this file as Nebula.psd.

3. Click on the foreground color and change the color to a light pink, RGB 228, 121, 149.

4. Double-click on the Airbrush tool to open its Options dialog box. Set the Airbrush Options to Normal and the Pressure to 21%. Change the brush to the following settings:
   - Diameter: 65 pixels
   - Hardness: 0%
   - Spacing: 25%
   - Default Angle and Roundness

5. Using the Airbrush, in the middle left of the Nebula layer, create some downward strokes, as shown in Figure 8.52.

Figure 8.52 The Nebula layer (with the star field showing through from the second layer) after adding downward Airbrush strokes.

6. Change the Airbrush Options to Multiply, and add a few more dark strokes to the nebula cloud.

7. Double-click on the Burn tool icon. Set the Burn tool Options to Midtones and its Exposure to 50%. Change the brush to the following settings:
   - Diameter: 13 pixels
   - Hardness: 0%
   - Spacing: 25%
   - Default Angle and Roundness

8. Use the Burn tool to make some marks like those shown in Figure 8.53.

9. Double-click on the Smudge tool. Set it to Normal with a Pressure of 62%. Then, use the following brush settings:
   - Diameter: 35 pixels
   - Hardness: 0%
   - Spacing: 25%
   - Default Angle and Roundness

   After you push and pull the colors with the Smudge tool, the image should look something like Figure 8.54.

10. Change the foreground color to white, RGB 255, 255, 255.

Figure 8.53 The image after making some marks with the Burn tool.

Figure 8.54 The nebula image after pushing and pulling the color around with the Smudge tool.

11. Double-click on the Airbrush tool to open its Options dialog box. Set the Airbrush Options to Normal and the Pressure to 21%. Change the brush to the following settings:

   • Diameter: 65 pixels

   • Hardness: 0%

   • Spacing: 25%

   • Default Angle and Roundness

12. Using the Airbrush, paint a big white splotch at the top of the nebula, as shown in Figure 8.55.

13. Double-click on the Smudge tool again. Set it to Normal with a Pressure of 62%, and use the following brush settings:

   • Diameter: Alternate between a brush that is 23 pixels and one that is 9 pixels

   • Hardness: 0%

   • Spacing: 25%

   • Default Angle and Roundness

14. Change the foreground color to a blue, RGB 106, 216, 252.

15. Double-click on the Airbrush tool to open its Options dialog box. Set the Airbrush Options to Overlay and the Pressure to 6%. Change the brush to the following settings:

Figure 8.55   The image after adding the white to the top of the nebula with the Airbrush.

- Diameter: 65 pixels
- Hardness: 0%
- Spacing: 25%
- Default Angle and Roundness

16. Using this Airbrush, paint in some cloud areas of blue surrounding the white areas and the perimeter of the nebula, as shown in Figure 8.56.

17. Change the foreground color to a very bright yellow, RGB 255, 253, 198.

18. Select the Airbrush tool. Set the Airbrush Options to Normal with a Pressure of 22%. Change the brush to the following settings:
    - Diameter: 65 pixels
    - Hardness: 0%
    - Spacing: 25%
    - Default Angle and Roundness

19. Add the light yellow color to the outer edges of the white part of the nebula, as shown in Figure 8.57.

20. Change the foreground color to a chocolate brown, RGB 87, 36, 33.

Figure 8.56 The nebula after adding the blue with the Overlay Airbrush.

Figure 8.57 The image after adding some bright yellow surrounding the bright white area of the nebula.

21. Select the Airbrush tool. Set the Airbrush Options to Normal with a Pressure of 22%. Change the brush to the following settings:

    - Diameter: 5 pixels

    - Hardness: 0%

    - Spacing: 25%

    - Default Angle and Roundness

22. Paint some small lines in the upper left of the bright area of the nebula, as shown in Figure 8.58.

23. Select the Smudge tool again. Set it to Normal with a Pressure of 62%, and use the following brush settings:

    - Diameter: Alternate between a brush that is 9 pixels and one that is 23 pixels

    - Hardness: 0%

    - Spacing: 25%

    - Default Angle and Roundness

24. Using the Smudge tool, pull some of the pixels of the brown lines until you get an effect like that shown in Figure 8.59.

25. Select the Burn tool. Set it to Midtones with an Exposure of 50%, and use the following brush settings:

Figure 8.58 The nebula image after adding the brown marks with the Airbrush.

Figure 8.59 The image after smudging some of the brown lines.

- Diameter: 5 pixels
- Hardness: 0%
- Spacing: 25%
- Default Angle and Roundness

26. Using the Burn tool, darken the far right areas where you smudged the brown marks. Also, darken some of the areas of the nebula where swirls are occurring. Think of this step as attacking areas that look false to you—leaving alone the areas that look good (see Figure 8.60).

27. From the Layers panel or the Layer pull-down menu, select Flatten Image.

28. Because the nearest nebula is nearly six light years away, most likely you'll see stars in front of a nebula. To enhance the foreground star effect, select Filter|Render|Lens Flare. Then, set Brightness to 16 and lens type to 105 mm Prime. The final nebula image map should look something like Figure 8.61.

Take a look at Figure 8.62 to see what the spaceship that you have just created looks like when it's presented with the star field, planet, and the background nebula.

Figure 8.60 The nebula image after darkening a few areas with the Burn tool.

Figure 8.61 The final nebula image map after adding several lens flare effects (see figure in Color Studio).

Figure 8.62 The culmination of your image-mapping endeavors to create a photorealistic science fiction scene (see figure in Color Studio).

Moving On

Science fiction films and television series have inundated American culture. One of the results in recent years is that visual effects have undergone a drastic increase in viewer appreciation. Today, viewers expect much more of visual-effects artists. To meet the expectations of the viewers, digital artists must continually increase their artistic skills. Science fiction scenes are a great proving ground for the budding 3D artist. I hope that this chapter has brought you closer to achieving the imagery that you want to achieve. In the next chapter, you'll be introduced to one of the most challenging of all the 3D surfacing tasks: painting organic creature textures.

PAINTING ORGANIC
CREATURE TEXTURES

9

One of the most fascinating aspects of 3D computer graphics is the ability it gives you to design and create fully realized, photorealistic 3D creatures. Of course, this is also one of the most challenging aspects that a 3D artist faces, because real-world creatures are rather complex. Mother Nature doesn't scrimp on details, so you can't afford to either.

The most ambitious surfacing challenges concern organic creatures and humans, because we are constantly looking at skin, whether it's our own or somebody else's. We take it for granted, but we know exactly what skin looks like—when it's cold, if it's sore, and when it's sickly. If you think about it, it's pretty amazing just how much detail we have stored up about the appearance of skin. So why all this talk about skin? Simple, because that's the main component of organic creatures.

To get your 3D creations to leap off the screen with lifelike realism, they need to be meticulously modeled and their skin needs to look as though it belongs in the real world. Why spend hours or months creating the coolest looking, drop-dead creature anyone has ever seen, only to stamp a boring shader onto its surface? Sounds ludicrous, right? But that seems to be the common practice. If you want to make your organic creatures come to life, you need to give them lifelike surfaces. So how can you do this armed only with Photoshop and your 3D program? In this chapter, you'll learn the following elements of creature surfacing:

- Realistic skin textures, color depth, veins, and wrinkles
- Specularity mapping
- Pimples and warts
- Pores and pock marks
- Eyes, teeth, scars, bones, tendons, fingernails, muscles
- Slime

Well that's quite a list, so we'd better get started.

Realistic Skin Textures

Whether you're surfacing a frog, a human, or an alien from the planet Zarvax, you want the skin to look realistic. Even if the creature isn't naked, it's the skin that attracts the most attention. So you want to make that skin as realistic as possible. You want the viewer to know, merely by looking at the creature, just how the skin feels. Is it soft and clammy, or smooth and silky? Is it hard and dry, or sticky and slimy?

In this section, you take a look at how to create the skin textures on a 3D creature named Gorg. But first, let's get to know him a little better.

Getting To Know Gorg

Gorg represents the culmination of a muscle-bound human and a Uromastyx lizard (an Egyptian desert lizard). He stands approximately 12 inches tall and weighs in at just over 16 ounces. He's approximately 22 years old in Gorg years, which would make him about 108 in human years.

As creatures go, Gorg is one tough dude. He's extremely strong and very fast. He's also endowed with fierce claws and extremely sharp teeth, but Gorg's main means of defense comes from having an incredibly tough skull, which he uses like a battering ram to rupture the internal organs of his opponent.

Because you'll be surfacing Gorg's thick skull, you must communicate to the viewer just what his skull is made of, what it feels like, how it reacts to light, where it's been, and what type of geography it was designed for. It seems like a big job, but it's well worth the struggle. Take a look at Figure 9.1, which shows Gorg without any image maps.

Gorg has been meticulously modeled to withstand even the harshest of environments. His neck is nearly as thick as his waist! He's a very tough little creature, so what you need to do is to find Gorg's visual counterpart from within Mother Nature's vast library of biological examples. You need to create image maps that convince the viewer Gorg's head is capable of knocking down a brick wall and coming out the other side unscathed.

Figure 9.1 Gorg with no texture maps.

Acquiring Reference Material

After searching far and wide to find a lizard that will be an appropriate fit for Gorg's head, you might discover the Uromastyx lizard, shown in Figure 9.2.

This is the scanned image of the Uromastyx lizard. Your job is to put the skin of the Uromastyx onto the figure of Gorg. You could have searched far and wide for good photos of the Uromastyx, but fortunately we had an actual Uromastyx handy. Of course, if you don't happen to have one of these endangered species handy, the children's section of the public library is the best alternative.

Once in the children's section, you'll want to look for the *Eyewitness Books* or the *Look Closer* series. Whether you're creating creatures, cities, or biplanes, these books are an extraordinary source of spectacular

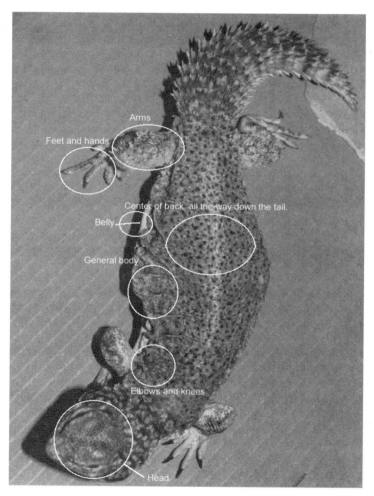

Figure 9.2 The resource image of the Uromastyx lizard.

visual reference. You'll find a detailed listing of wonderful source material books in Appendix A, in the back of this book.

Because Gorg is such a muscle-bound creature, you need to find some reference imagery of big, buff, body building dudes. For these images, you don't need to go any further than the local supermarket magazine rack, where you can find muscle mags galore. These magazines give you all the reference material you need for creating muscle and vein maps for Gorg.

Now that you have acquired all the best reference material you can carry, you are ready to start putting it all together.

Putting It All Together

At this point, you need to start choosing the specific elements from your reference material to incorporate into Gorg's surfaces. These are elements that stand out, the ones that really catch the eye. Because you are dealing with a fantasy creature, you are free to mix and match the most inspiring elements from your resource material.

To expedite things, stick to surfacing only the head. Gorg will be covered with scales, so let's create some skin texture by incorporating scales. First, you need to figure out the best technique to use for seamlessly applying scales to the entirety of Gorg's skin.

Preparing Gorg For The Scales

To create seamless, tileable image maps that cover Gorg's entire skin, you need to have a place to put them. So, you need to define the surfaces on Gorg's head. First, in your 3D program, load the Gorg object from the chapt9\Gorg folder on the companion CD-ROM. The model is provided in a number of file formats, so select the one that's compatible with your program.

After it's loaded, select the skin surrounding Gorg's head, but be sure *not* to select Gorg's teeth, eyes, nostrils, tongue, or his gums. (Scaly teeth are not the most attractive things you'll ever see.)

When the skin surrounding his entire head is selected, name this area Skin, or something imaginative like that. Now, simply save the model as Gorgnew and you're ready to get started on the scales. Getting the scales to cover Gorg's head could turn into a real surfacing nightmare if not handled properly. To get all of those scales to exactly match up with one another and still have a seamless surface with no texture map stretching, use the cubic mapping method. Cubic mapping allows

CHOOSING A COMPATIBLE FORMAT FOR GORGHEAD

The Gorg files on the CD come in the following file formats:

- *3DMF*—Apple QuickDraw 3D format.

- *DXF*—The most common format that just about any 3D program can open.

- *LWO*—Stands for LightWave Object and is the LightWave 3D format.

- *MAX*—3D Studio MAX format.

- *WAV*—Alias/Wavefront format.

you to map one image equally to all six sides of an object, even if that object is organic in shape like Gorg's head. Take a look at Figure 9.3 to get a better idea of how cubic mapping works.

As you can see, a cubic map does a great job of applying basic surfaces to organic objects.

Because the scales appear as little bumps on a creature's skin, let's get started by making the bump map for the scales first. To make this bump map a repeating, tileable map that allows you to completely cover Gorg's head (and body) with a seamless scale pattern, you have to follow a few simple steps to get this to work. Let's get started.

Creating A Seamless, Tileable, Bump Map For Gorg's Scales

1. Open Photoshop and create a 500×500-pixel image with a white background. Make sure that black is the foreground color and white is in the background.

2. Select the stained glass filter under Filter|Texture|Stained Glass and apply the following settings in the dialog box:
   - Cell Size: 10
   - Border Thickness: 4
   - Light Intensity: 7

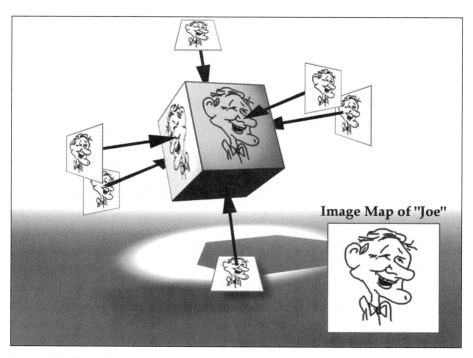

Figure 9.3 The cubic mapping method.

The result of this operation should look like Figure 9.4.

3. This gives you a nice, chaotic pattern with a black border surrounding it, but you're not quite there yet. You have to get rid of this black border by cropping the image.

4. Using the Cropping tool, select an area about four or eight pixels in from the outer edges. You want to have just half a scale at the edges so the image is seamlessly tileable. When you get the right placement, hit Return (Mac) or Enter (Windows) to crop the image, as shown in Figure 9.5.

5. You need to soften these scales a bit in order to give them a wider range of gray, so the bump isn't too sharp. This prevents Gorg's scales from looking like they were created with a cookie cutter. To do this, select the Gaussian Blur filter and set the Radius to 3.1.

6. Select Image|Adjust|Brightness/Contrast and set the Brightness to -55 and Contrast to +39 to increase the contrast and prevent the scales from looking too washed out. It's still a little too gray. You need to have the highlights really stand out, so that your scale bumps actually look like bumps and not a smooth surface.

7. Select the Magic Wand tool, set a tolerance of 20, and click on the highlight (the light areas) of one of these bumps. Then, choose Select|Similar to select all the center highlight areas of this image map, as shown in Figure 9.6.

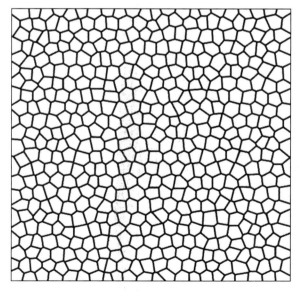

Figure 9.4 The basic scale pattern.

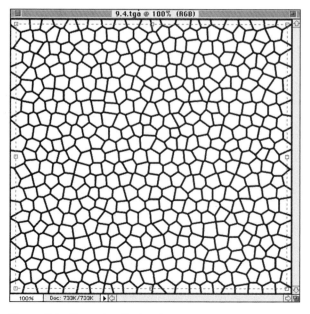

Figure 9.5 Removing the border.

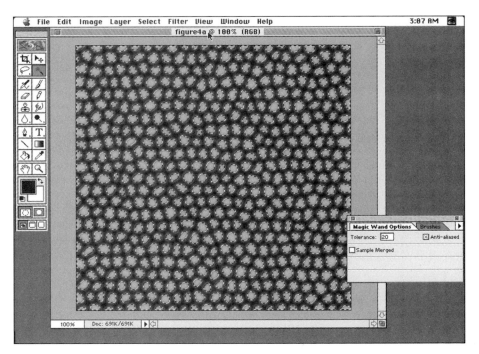

Figure 9.6 Selecting the highlights.

8. Hide the distracting, little marching ants by choosing: View|Hide Edges. You need to soften the edges of this selection a bit though. Choose Select|Feather and set the Feather Radius to 2 pixels. Now, select the Image|Adjust|Brightness/Contrast again and set the Brightness to +57 and the Contrast to +37.

That looks good, but you still can't use this as a tileable image map because all of its outer edges are still different from one another. That's not difficult to change, so let's take a look at how to make this image tileable.

Turning The Scale Pattern Into A Tileable Image Map

1. Using the square selection tool, make a 40-pixel-wide selection on the outer edge of the left side. Then, copy and paste it, creating a new layer. Now, select Layer|Transform|Flip Horizontal. While holding down the Shift key (to constrain the layers movement), slide the layer over to the extreme right edge of the image map, as shown in Figure 9.7.

As you can see, the scale pattern on the outer left edge doesn't quite match up with the rest of your image map.

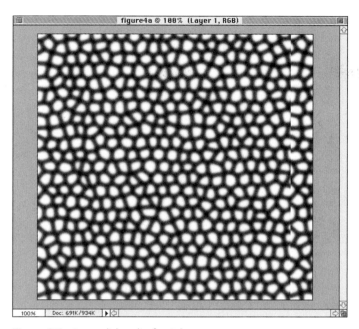

Figure 9.7   Layer slid to the far right.

2.   To fix this problem, select the Erasure tool (or hit the E key on your keyboard). Set it to an airbrush in the Options palette with a pressure of 63%, a diameter of about 20 pixels, and a hardness of 0. Then, begin to remove that edge a little bit at a time, creating complete scales as you move the eraser. Of course, it doesn't always work out that way, but you can fix those little imperfections with the paint tools. After you've erased the hard edge, flatten the layers by choosing Layer|Flatten Image.

3.   To fix the areas where the size and shape of the scales have become distorted, use a white airbrush with the pressure set to about 26%, a brush diameter of about 13 pixels and a hardness of 5%.

4.   To complete the bump map, repeat Steps 1 through 6 for the vertical section.

Now that you're finished creating the tileable bump map for Gorg's scales, you need to give it the tile test in Photoshop.

The Photoshop Tile Test

1.   Make sure that your image has been flattened. If it isn't, select Layer|Flatten Image.

2.   Choose Select|Select All and define this selection as a pattern by selecting Edit|Define Pattern.

3. Because you're dealing with an image that's 500×500 pixels, you want to create a new image that's twice its size. That way, you can see how all edges of this image meet up with one another. Select File|New and enter a width and height of 1,000 pixels.

4. Select Edit|Fill and enter the following values in the dialog box:

   • Use: Pattern

   • Opacity: 100%

   • Mode: Normal

   Figure 9.8 shows the result of this operation.

If there are any noticeable problems concerning how the image is tiling, you'll need to go back to the image (just before the tile test) and fix any trouble areas with Photoshop's painting tools. Figure 9.9 shows what the final bump map should look like.

Now that you have a perfectly seamless, tileable bump map for Gorg's scales, you can begin making your accompanying diffusion and specularity maps. Fortunately, you can use the bump map you just created for the foundation of these image maps.

A Scale Diffusion Map

You can create a diffusion map by simply duplicating the bump map you just made and making some minor changes to it. Let's get started.

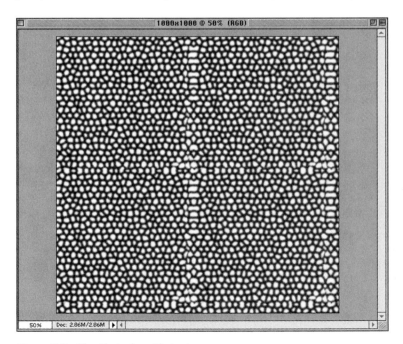

Figure 9.8 The Photoshop tile test.

Creating A Diffusion Map

1. Select the bump map layer you just made and duplicate it.

2. Select Image|Adjust|Brightness/Contrast and enter the following values:
   - Brightness: +85
   - Contrast: -85

3. You should now have something similar to Figure 9.10. Name this layer Diffusion and save the Photoshop file.

Now, you need to create the scale specularity map.

The Scale Specularity Map

You could simply place a global specularity value on the scales, but that wouldn't appear very natural because there is a great deal of variance in specularity across the surface of the scales. Fortunately, the specularity map is relatively simple to create; you merely need to modify the bump map image. Let's do this now.

Creating A Specularity Map

1. Make another copy of the bump map layer by duplicating it. Name this layer Specularity.

   You need to lower both the Brightness and Contrast of this layer or the specularity will be too high, which makes the scales much too shiny.

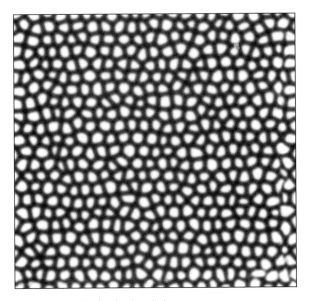

Figure 9.9 The finished scale bump map.

Figure 9.10 The scale diffusion map.

2. Select Image|Adjust|Brightness/Contrast and add these values:
   - Brightness: -100
   - Contrast: -90

Finally, you need to export each of the image maps as separate files. Select the entire image (whether it's the bump, diffusion, or specularity layer) by choosing Select|All. Copy this layer. Now, select a new file and paste the layer into the new file. Save the new file as Gorgscalebump, Gorgscalediff, or so on.

That's all there is to creating photorealistic scale maps that are both seamless and tileable. Now, let's apply these maps to Gorg's head. But first, you need to prepare the model for the application of these maps.

Preparing Gorg's Head For Cubic Mapping

1. Open the file called Gorg1, which can be found in Models\chapt9models\Gorg on the companion CD-ROM. Select the 3D file format that your 3D program can read.

2. Select all of the skin on Gorg's head, leaving the teeth, eyes, gums, and tongue alone.

3. Save the skin selection.

4. Load the bump, specularity, and diffusion maps that you just made into your 3D program.

5. Cubic map each of the scale image maps onto Gorg's skin. Be sure to keep the repeating tile sizes the same for each of these image maps so that they line up exactly with one another.

Take a look at Figure 9.11 to see what Gorg should look like once the scale maps have been applied to his head with the cubic mapping method.

Now that you've got Gorg looking scaly, you're ready to begin applying some color depth to this creature.

Applying Color Depth

Achieving photorealistic color depth really results from the culmination of all image mapping techniques. When color, diffusion, specularity, and bump mapping are successfully combined, the results can be incredibly realistic. As you can see from Figure 9.11, the scales really seem to be working well, but the model lacks realism. It still looks like a computer-generated graphic. One way that you can help to remedy this situation is to create realistic color depth. To do this, you need to refer back to your photographic reference material.

Back To The Reference Material

Figure 9.12 shows some of the reference images that give you an idea of what Gorg's surfacing should look like. If you want to achieve photo-realism, it helps to have some good reference photos to guide you.

You're going to need some good templates of Gorg's head, so you know just where to apply the color. You don't want the dark circles under Gorg's eyes to end up on his chin. Let's take a look at how you go about creating these templates.

Figure 9.11   Gorg's head with scale maps applied.

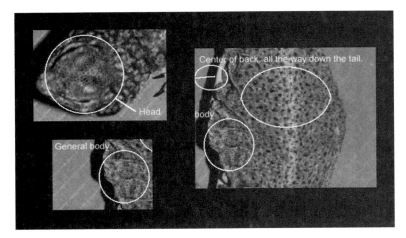

Figure 9.12   The reference material for creating realistic color depth.

Note: *If your 3D program allows you to render from the orthographic view, make sure to apply different colors to the front, sides, top, and back portions of the skin selections. This ensures that you can easily tell where one portion ends and another begins. If you can't render from one of the orthographic views, it's a good idea to do some renderings from the perspective view. Just be sure to set the zoom on your camera to around 800, which flattens out the perspective of the model, so it matches the wireframe image. You need to have rendered versions of the head so you'll be able to tell exactly where the lips, eyes, nose, ears, and other features are located on the model, which will be valuable when you begin painting these details.*

Preparing Gorg's Head For Planar Mapping

1. In your modeling program, open the Gorg model from the Models\chapt9models\Gorg directory on the companion CD-ROM. This is the model that has the scales attached.

2. Because you'll be using planar mapping to surface Gorg's head, you're going to need to split his head into its respective planes. That is, the front, side, back, and the top of the model, as shown in Figure 9.13.

3. Once you've got each of the sides selected, give them a unique name and save the model as Gorgplane.

4. Begin rendering out some templates of Gorg's head that you'll use for reference when painting the maps later. Render the front, sides, top, and back from the orthographic view if your 3D program allows you to do this. If not, you'll need to screen capture the wire frame images from your modeling program. Figure 9.14 shows the side template for Gorg's head.

After you've rendered out all of your templates, you're ready to begin painting. First, load the views into Photoshop. Then, crop each of these template images to the border of the selection you want to paint. See Figure 9.15.

Now, you're ready to start painting the color depth on Gorg's face.

Painting Gorg's Image Maps

You'll need to find a good base color for Gorg's head. This is kind of like preparing a canvas with a base coat of paint.

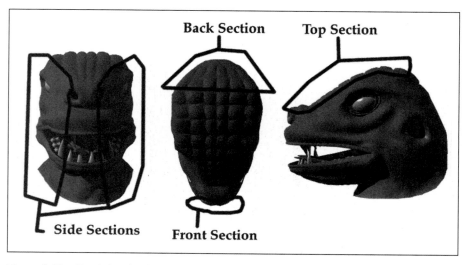

Figure 9.13 Gorg's head split up into planes.

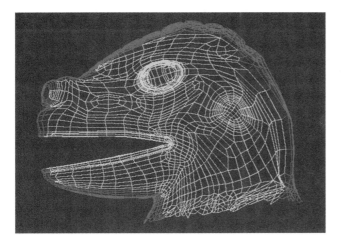

Note: *If your 3D application doesn't allow you to use diffusion maps, simply ignore Steps 5 through 7.*

Figure 9.14 Wireframe view of Gorg's head.

Painting Gorg's Base Color

1. To find a good base color, take a look at the reference image of your Uromastyx lizard again. See Figure 9.16.

2. After you've selected the base color RGB 198, 176, 135 with the Eyedropper tool (or by clicking on the foreground color and setting it to RGB 198, 176, 135), create a new layer named Color. Then, select all and fill this layer with the new base color.

3. Select Image|Adjust|Brightness/Contrast and set the Brightness to +35 (leave the contrast alone). The reason you must increase the brightness of the base color is to compensate for the diffusion map that you'll be creating.

4. Create a new layer named Diffusion.

5. While in this new diffusion layer, click on the color swatch and set it to RGB 191, 191, 191. Then, fill the new layer with this color.

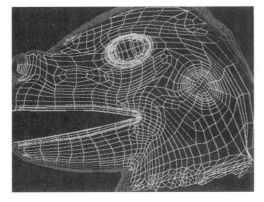

Figure 9.15 The side view template cropped down to the selection area.

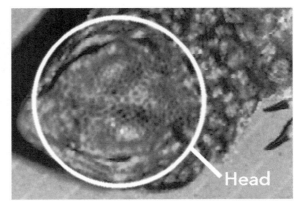

Figure 9.16 The undertone color for Gorg (see figure in Color Studio).

6. Copy each of these layers to separate files. Save the color map as Gorgsidecolor and the diffusion map as Gorgsidediffusion. This is also a good time to save the entire Photoshop document as Gorgsidehead.psd.

7. In your 3D application, load both the color and diffusion image maps and map them to your model, so you can see what this base color looks like. Now, render out a test image of Gorg's head, as shown in Figure 9.17.

Now, open this test render in Photoshop and compare it with the reference image of your Uromastyx lizard. You might need to adjust the base color a bit to match the source image. When you've gotten a good match between your test render and the reference image, you are ready to move on to creating some skin details.

Skin Detail

Now that you've got a good base color for Gorg, you can begin to create the skin details, which transport Gorg out of the computer graphics world and into reality.

Figure 9.17 The combination of color and diffusion mapping.

Painting Gorg's Skin Details

1. Referring once again to the reference image of the Uromastyx lizard, you need to find a good skin pattern to use for Gorg's head. Figure 9.18 shows the area that should serve your purpose nicely.

2. Start with the side image map for Gorg's head. First, you need to select a good base gray color. Set the foreground color to RGB 45, 47, 51. Be sure to write down these RGB values because you'll also use this bluish gray color at the extreme edge of each of the four views (front, side, back, and top) to make the surfaces seamless.

3. Create an airbrush by double-clicking on the Airbrush icon in the toolbox and apply the following settings in the Airbrush Tool Options:

   - Diameter: 20 pixels

   - Hardness: 0%

   - Spacing: 5%

   - Pressure: 36%

   - Default Angle and Roundness

4. Keeping your fingers on the Undo keys—Command+Z (Mac) and Ctrl+Z (Windows), test this airbrush and color in the color layer just to get the look and feel of it.

5. Set the color layer opacity to 50%. The reason you need to make this layer transparent is so that you can see exactly where you'll be applying the color on your template. Now, spread the grayish blue color from just after Gorg's nose to the back of his head, as shown in Figure 9.19.

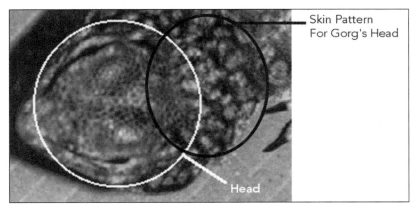

Figure 9.18 Reference skin pattern for Gorg's head.

Be sure to set airbrush pressure to 100% when painting on the edges of the template, so it seamlessly merges with the other image maps.

6. Add some white spots on top of the gray color to create a pattern like the one on Uromastyx's back (see Figure 9.20). You can see that many of the spots covering this area are almost white, so create the spot color using RGB 207, 207, 209 with these airbrush settings:

   - Pressure: 36%
   - Diameter: 13 pixels
   - Hardness: 5%

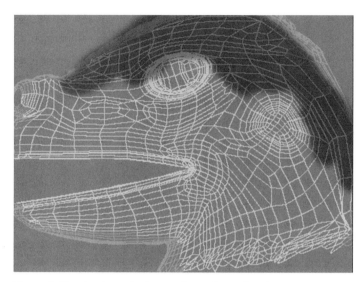

Figure 9.19 Applying the base color to Gorg's head.

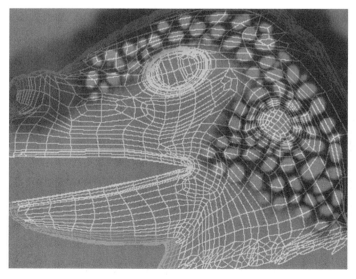

Figure 9.20 Looking through the color layer to the template image.

- Spacing: 5%
- Default Roundness and Angle

7. Set the color layer opacity to about 50%, as shown in Figure 9.20.

8. You can now begin adding the white spots to Gorg's head. To avoid seam problems, be sure not to put any white spots on the boundaries of the color map. To see where the boundary edge is, take a look at Figure 9.21.

9. After creating the spots, you need to break up their consistency with some smaller details, as shown in Figure 9.22. I've also added more spot patterns around Gorg's eye area and lips.

In the previous project, you only covered the planar mapping of one side of Gorg's head, but the concepts can be applied to the mapping of the front, top, and back of Gorg's head. Figure 9.23 shows what the final results look like after applying the color map you just made along with the scales you made in the first part of this chapter. You also added bump maps and diffusion maps to the head, which we'll be getting into in greater detail later in this chapter.

Another great way to add photorealism to creatures is by adding wrinkles to their skin. Wrinkles can give the illusion of age and can also add that extra spark of detail to the skin's surface that helps make the model stand out as a super-realistic 3D creation. Let's try your hand at creating wrinkles.

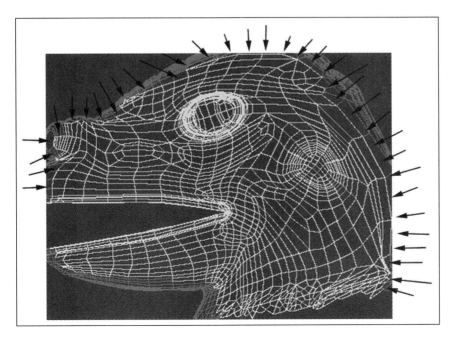

Figure 9.21 The boundary of your color map.

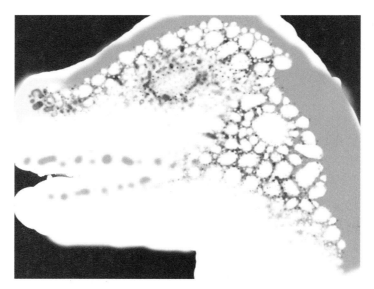

Figure 9.22 The final color map for the side of Gorg's head (see figure in Color Studio).

Figure 9.23 The final rendered image of the side of Gorg's head (see figure in Color Studio).

Wrinkled Skin Bump Maps

You could model the wrinkles on your creatures, but if you're like me, you can't afford to spend five months modeling one character. The more practical option is to use a bump map. To illustrate this technique, let's planar-map facial wrinkles onto a character named Dr. Dread.

Getting To Know Dr. Dread

Dr. Dread is sort of a cross between Dr. Frankenstein and Christopher Walken. He is extremely intelligent, but slightly unhinged. He's what is known as a "Living Toon," with the exaggerated features of a cartoon and the photorealistic details of a human. You're going to add some of those photorealistic details to Dr. Dread in the next few projects. Let's get started with his wrinkles.

Putting Some Wrinkles On Dr. Dread

It's always a good idea to pick up some worthy reference material. I found a great old family photo to refer to (see Figure 9.24).

Creating realistic wrinkles requires quality source material. Let's get started adding wrinkles to Dr. Dread's face.

Figure 9.24 The reference image for wrinkles.

Creating Wrinkled Skin

1. Open the template file Dreadface.psd, located in the chapt9\
   Dr. Dread folder on the companion CD-ROM.

2. Create a new layer and name it Bump.

3. Fill this layer with a gray color RGB 102, 102, 102. Now, select the
   Dodge tool with the Toning Tool Options set to Midtones, an ex-
   posure of 13%, and the following brush settings:
   - Diameter: 54 pixels
   - Hardness: 0%
   - Spacing: 5%
   - Default Angle and Roundness

4. Test out these Dodge tool settings before you make the bump
   layer semitransparent. When you're happy with the dodge tool
   settings, make the bump layer opacity 64%.

5. Using the Dodge tool, begin painting the areas where the wrinkles
   would protrude from Dr. Dread's forehead, as shown in Figure 9.25.

6. Select the Burn tool with Toning Tool Options set to Midtones,
   Exposure of 36%, and the brush settings:
   - Diameter: 5 pixels

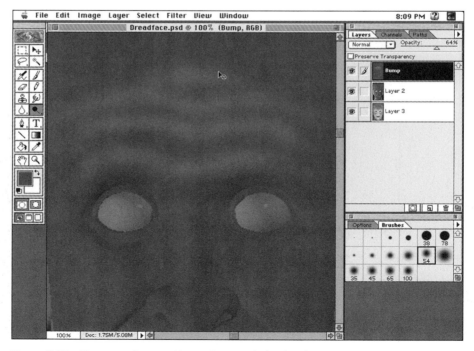

Figure 9.25 The protruding wrinkles on Dr. Dread's forehead.

- Hardness: 0%
- Spacing: 3%
- Default Angle and Roundness

7. Using this smaller brush, darken the areas that lie between the raised areas you just painted. These lines create the creases of Dr. Dread's forehead. Take a look at Figure 9.26, which illustrates this operation.

8. Create some wrinkles around the good doctor's eyes, mouth, and cheeks. A good rule of thumb when painting wrinkles is to try to follow the contours of the model's face. Try to imagine where the wrinkles would naturally occur on his face if he were smiling, frowning, grimacing, and so on. Be sure to frequently reference your source material. You should have something similar to Figure 9.27 when you're finished.

Creating realistic wrinkles is basically a matter of using the Burn and Dodge tools alternatively and adjusting the brush sizes and pressure settings so that you can paint the wrinkles to conform to Dr. Dread's face. Now, save the Photoshop file as Dreadface1.psd and save a copy of the bump map as DreadFaceWrinkle.TGA or some other file format that your 3D program can handle. Finally, you need to planar-map the image to the front of Dr. Dread's head.

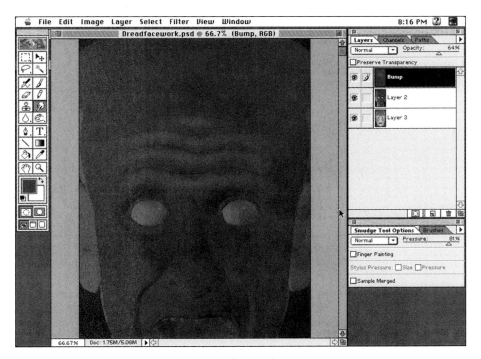

Figure 9.26   The dark creases in Dr. Dread's forehead.

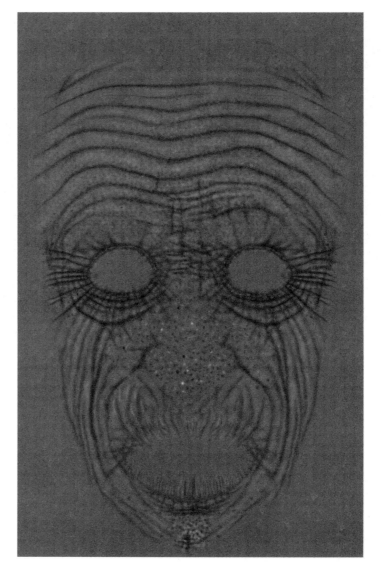

Figure 9.27 The final bump map for Dr. Dread's wrinkles.

Figure 9.28 shows what Dr. Dread should look like after you've planar-mapped these wrinkles to the front of his face. In this rendered image, diffusion and specularity maps have also been added to bring out the wrinkles a bit more. These maps can be found in DreadFace2.psd on the companion CD-ROM in the chapt9\Dr. Dread folder.

Now that you understand wrinkle mapping a little better, let's add a few more integral details to Dr. Dread's face. One of the facial details almost always overlooked when it comes to surfacing a 3D character's face is the existence of pores. If you have skin, you have pores—after

Figure 9.28   The final render of Dr. Dread's wrinkles (see figure in Color Studio).

all, the skin needs to breathe. So if you want to create creatures and characters that look like they're alive, they need to have pores.

Forming Realistic Skin

Many people wish that they had perfectly smooth, unmarked skin like the faces that grace the covers of glamour magazines. But even those faces are not perfect. They've been touched up by an artist with an airbrush so that you cannot see the pock marks, wrinkles and pores. If you want your characters and creatures to look real, they cannot have perfectly smooth skin. They may not need to have a face covered with pimples, but they do need to have pores.

Pores And Pockmarks

Pores are basically indentations in the skin. When these indentations become really noticeable or exaggerated, you call them pockmarks. Pockmarks are usually caused by a bad case of acne that has been picked at or has become infected. Well, you needn't get into all of the gory details here. Suffice it to say that pockmarks are really big pores. Let's take a look at how do you go about creating pores and pockmarks on your 3D creations.

Creating Skin Pores

1. Open Dreadface1.psd in chapt9\Dr_Dread on the CD-ROM. This is the file that you created the bump map wrinkles for.

2. Jump into the bump map layer—the wrinkle map should still be there.

3. Select Photoshop's Burn tool and set it to Midtones, with an exposure of 66%, and the following brush settings:

   - Diameter: 5 pixels
   - Hardness: 26%
   - Spacing: 420%
   - Default Angle and Roundness

4. Don't forget to test this brush out to get the feel of it before you change the bump map's opacity to 64%.

5. Begin creating the pores for your bump map. Try not to allow the pores to bunch up or become too concentrated in any one area. Keeping the mouse button pressed, spread the dots out evenly, especially on Dr. Dread's forehead, chin, and nose areas. See Figure 9.29.

6. Make the bump map layer 100 percent visible by setting its opacity to 100%.

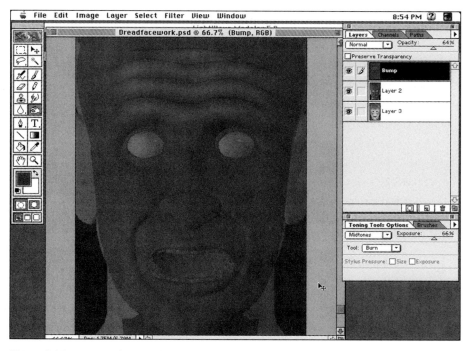

Figure 9.29 Dr. Dread's pores bump map.

7. Leave the Burn tools exposure at 66%, but change its brush settings to:

   - Diameter: 10 pixels
   - Hardness: 8%
   - Spacing: 4%
   - Default Angle and Roundness

   You'll use this new Burn brush to change some of Dr. Dread's pores into pockmarks. The best areas for creating this effect are around Dr. Dread's nose and cheek areas.

8. Notice how the pores become pockmarks as your new Burn brush appears to open up and spread out the pores. Go over some of Dr. Dread's original pores with the Burn brush and these pores will become pockmarks.

Now that you have skin pores, you are ready for a little more detail. To justify the pockmarks, you should add some pimples. Let's take a look at how this is done.

Pimples And Warts

Basically, creating pimples and warts is just the opposite of creating pores and pockmarks, except that generally, warts and pimples are not as plentiful as pores. If you want to give Dr. Dread a good case of acne, you had better begin in the bump map layer of your template.

Creating Skin Abnormalities (Pimples)

1. Create a Dodge brush with an exposure setting of 82% and the following Brush settings:

   - Diameter: 10 pixels
   - Hardness: 5%
   - Spacing: 5%
   - Default Angle and Roundness

2. Give the bump map layer an opacity of 64%.

3. Add a few dabs in the places where you want pimples and warts to occur on Dr. Dread's face. Just keep in mind that the more you dodge (meaning the lighter the area gets), the larger that particular pimple or wart will become on Dr. Dread's skin. As for the placement of these pimples and warts, apply them over the character's nose and forehead. To see where to place the pimples, it's probably best to check out some reference photos—like an old high school yearbook.

4. If you really want to set off these warts and pimples, you can create specularity and diffusion maps for them. To create the specularity map, duplicate the Bump layer, rename it Specularity, and change the Image|Adjust|Brightness/Contrast to Brightness: -92, Contrast: -85. The results should look like Figure 9.30.

5. Notice that the areas around Dr. Dread's eyes, nose, and lips have also been lightened. This is to increase the shininess (specularity) in those areas of the face that are naturally more oil producing and shiny. To do this, simply change the brush settings on the Dodge tool to:

   - Exposure 33%
   - Diameter: 100 pixels
   - Hardness: 0%
   - Spacing: 25%
   - Default Angle and Roundness

6. Make another duplicate of the Bump and name the new layer Diffusion. Select Brightness/Contrast and change the Brightness to 100% and the Contrast to -72%. Take a look at Figure 9.31.

7. To make these pimples and warts stand out as photorealistic blemishes, give them a little color. Start by creating a new layer for Dr. Dread and name it Color.

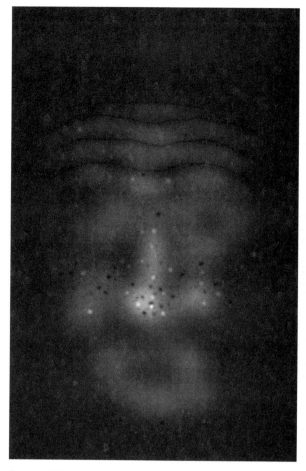

Figure 9.30 The specularity map for Dr. Dread's pimples and pockmarks.

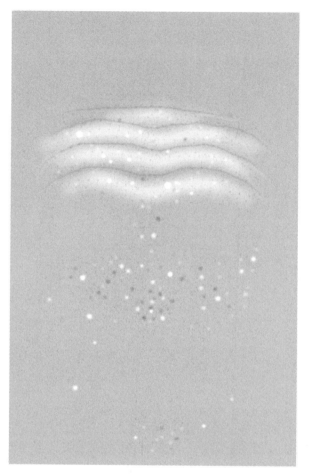

Figure 9.31 The diffusion map for Dr. Dread's pimples and pockmarks.

8. Fill this layer with a base skin color of RGB 197, 124, 87.

9. Select a good pimple color, like RGB 197, 93, 53 and create an airbrush with the following settings:

   - Pressure 15%
   - Diameter: 13 pixels
   - Hardness: 5%
   - Spacing: 5%
   - Default Angle and Roundness

10. Make the color layer about 70% transparent with the bump map layer visible beneath it so you can see the pimples you'll be coloring.

To see what a really pimply faced Dr. Dread looks like, export the layers as individual files and map them to your Dr. Dread head model. It should look something like Figure 9.32.

Figure 9.32   Dr. Dread with acne.

It's the little surfacing details that bring a character to life. Now, let's move on to something that's a little less gruesome—creating creature's eyes.

Eyes And Teeth

Did you ever notice that when you're talking with people, you mainly watch their eyes and mouth? I guess it's human nature. But for this reason, you need to make your character/creature's eyes and teeth as realistic as possible because they are going to be receiving the most attention from the viewer—especially if the character/creature is going to be speaking.

The Eyes Have It

When you look at someone, the first thing that you tend to notice is the eyes. I don't care if that someone has five horns and a beak, their eyes will generally get the most attention. This being the case, you want to make sure that the eyes are as realistic as possible. As always, it's a good idea to pick up some good reference material for the eyes. Or better yet, a mirror. Let's give Dr. Dread some haunting eyes.

Creating Creature Eyes

1. Open the Dreadeye.psd Photoshop file in the chapt9\Dr. Dread folder. This is the template for the doctor's eyes.

2. Create a new color layer. Fill this layer with a good eye white color RGB 253, 234, 215 and name it Color.

3. Create another layer to be used for creating the pupil of the eye.

4. Using the elliptical selection tool, hold down the Shift key (to keep the circle a perfect circle) and define the area of the actual eyeball. Take a look at Figure 9.33 to see the circle selection area.

5. Feather this circle selection by two pixels and then fill it with a blue color RGB 61, 107, 134.

6. To add the details to the iris of the eye, add some noise to the eye by selecting Filter|Noise|Amount: 27, Distribution: Gaussian, and make sure that the Monochromatic box is checked. This gives you some details in the iris.

7. Apply a blur filter (Blur|Radial Blur) to the noise with these settings.
   - Amount: 22
   - Blur Method: Zoom
   - Quality: Good

8. Usually the iris has a slightly darker color surrounding it. To create this effect, choose a slightly darker blue, such as RGB 20, 59, 109. Select Edit|Stroke and use the following settings:

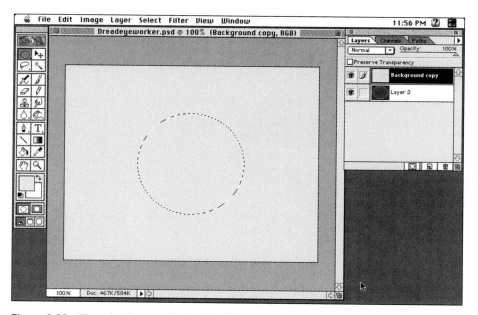

Figure 9.33 The selection area for the iris of the eye.

- Width: 5 pixels
- Location: Center
- Blending|Opacity: 100%
- Mode: Normal

9. Emphasize the details of the iris a bit more with the Unsharp Mask Filter with these settings:
    - Amount: 150%
    - Radius: 8.4 pixels
    - Threshold: 5 levels

10. For the pupil, select a black color by pushing the D key. (In Photoshop, the D key loads the default colors: black and white.)

11. Choose a paintbrush with the following settings:
    - Opacity: 100%
    - Diameter: 78 pixels
    - Hardness: 100%
    - Spacing: 25%
    - Default Angle and Roundness

12. Before adding the pupil, create a new layer for it and place a dot in the center of the iris with your new paintbrush.

13. If you find that the pupil isn't exactly in the center of the iris, position it with Photoshop's Move tool.

14. The eye isn't complete without a few blood-shot lines, so let's add a few. You need to exchange your paintbrush for an airbrush with the following settings:
    - Pressure: 29%
    - Diameter: 3 pixels
    - Hardness: 100%
    - Spacing: 25%
    - Default Angle and Roundness

15. Create a good red color for the bloodshot marks, such as RGB 225, 74, 60.

16. Add some meandering, vein-like squiggles onto the base color (white of the eye) area (see Figure 9.34).

The human eye is not actually a perfectly round ball like you might expect, but it has a slight bump on the iris. You can easily simulate this effect with a bump map.

Creating The Eye Bump Map

1. Create a new layer and name it "Bump".

2. Choose Select All and fill the layer with a gray base color RGB 102, 102, 102.

3. Be sure that this new "Bump" layer is on top of the "Color" layer. Set the "Bump" layer's opacity to about 70% so that the pupil can be seen beneath it.

4. Click on the foreground color and change it to white RGB 255, 255, 255. Set the airbrush tool to the following settings:
    - Pressure: 70%
    - Diameter: 172 pixels
    - Hardness: 0%
    - Spacing: 25%
    - Default Angle and Roundness

5. Spray the white color over the area where the pupil is.

The results should look like Figure 9.35.

Now, you simply need to export the color and bump layers. Then planar-map them to Dr. Dread's eyes. You should end up with something like Figure 9.36.

Now that you've given Dr. Dread some beautiful eyes, let's move on and create some planar maps for his teeth.

Realistic Teeth

If you want your characters and creatures to really look like movie stars, you need to give them some

Figure 9.34 The color map for Dr. Dread's eye (see figure in Color Studio).

Figure 9.35 The bump map for Dr. Dread's eye.

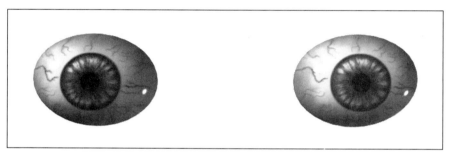

Figure 9.36 Dr. Dread's completed eyes.

great looking teeth. In order to create realistic teeth, you need to work on their color, texture, and shininess (or specularity).

Creating Teeth Textures

1. There's no better reference material than real life, so be sure to have a mirror handy when surfacing the teeth of Dr. Dread. Take a look at the Dreadteeth.psd Photoshop file located in chapt9\ Dr_Dread on the companion CD-ROM.

2. Create a new layer for the teeth color and title it Color. Dr. Dread spends many hours in the lab and drinks a lot of coffee, which subsequently stains his teeth. Because of that, give Dr. Dread's teeth a slightly off-white color.

3. Select all of the color layer and fill it with the base color RGB 241, 230, 197.

4. You need to add a few stains to Dr. Dread's teeth, so let's change the base color you just created to the new stain color RGB 167, 127, 58.

5. Select an airbrush and give it the following settings:

- Pressure: 13%
- Diameter: 36 pixels
- Hardness: 18%
- Spacing: 25%
- Default Angle and Roundness

6. Make the color layer semi-transparent, so you can see where to add color details to the teeth. Set the opacity for the layer to about 64%.

7. Using the airbrush, add some stains to Dr. Dread's teeth. Take a look at Figure 9.37 to see how the stains are applied.

Now that Dr. Dread's teeth are sufficiently stained, let's add a little texture to them with a new bump map layer.

Creating The Bump Map For Dr. Dread's Teeth

1. Create a new layer named Bump. Then, fill it with a gray color RGB 102,102, 102. Next, create a Burn brush to use when creating the darkened lines or grooves in Dr. Dread's teeth.

2. Select Photoshop's Burn tool and give the brush the following Toning Tool Options:
   - Exposure: 22%
   - Midtones
   - Diameter: 4 pixels
   - Hardness: 100%

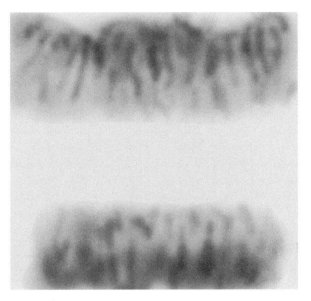

Figure 9.37 The stains on Dr. Dread's teeth.

- Spacing: 25%
- Default Angle and Roundness

3. Using the Burn tool, create vertical lines that begin at the base of each tooth and taper off as they reach the end of the tooth. To taper off the Burn tool lines, use Photoshop's Smudge tool with the following settings:

   - Pressure: 64%
   - Normal
   - Diameter: 13 pixels
   - Hardness: 5%
   - Spacing: 5%
   - Default Angle and Roundness

This gives Dr. Dread's teeth a realistic texture. Take a look at Figure 9.38 to see what the bump map should look like when you're finished.

You're almost done with the teeth. All you have left is the diffusion map for Dr. Dread's teeth, so let's get started on that.

Creating The Diffusion Map For Dr. Dread's Teeth

1. Begin the diffusion map by duplicating the bump map layer you just made and renaming it Diffusion.

2. Change the bump map layer's brightness and contrast by choosing Image|Adjust|Brightness/Contrast and giving it these settings: Brightness: +68, Contrast: -53.

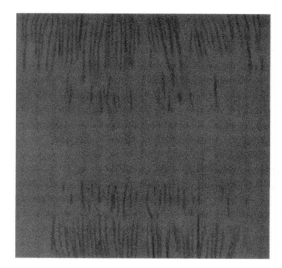

Figure 9.38 The bump map for Dr. Dread's teeth.

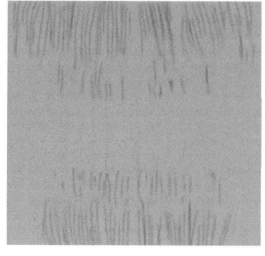

Figure 9.39 The diffusion map for Dr. Dread's teeth.

The results of this operation should resemble Figure 9.39.

Fortunately, you'll be able to also use this diffusion map for your specularity map of Dr. Dread's teeth. So, that's all there is to creating some photorealistic choppers for Dr. Dread. Take a look at Figure 9.40 to see Dr. Dread with the image maps applied to his teeth.

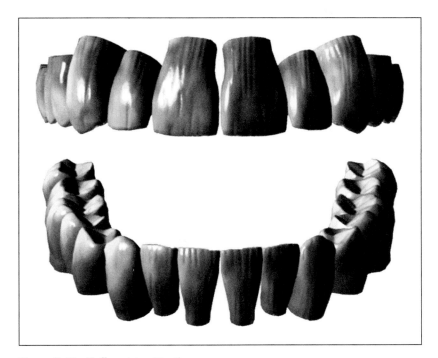

Figure 9.40 Coffee-stained teeth.

Now let's meet a new character that Dr. Dread created. This little guy was brought back to life in the good doctor's lab when Dr. Dread realized that he needed a helping hand.

Getting To Know Scratch

When Svenstein Schostakowski's private jet went down in the Alps several years ago, the only salvageable part of his body was his hand. Dr. Dread, being an avid Schostakowski fan and a remarkable surgeon, decided to bring the hand back to life as Scratch (see Figure 9.41).

One of the features that really adds to the realism of Scratch is the veins covering the back of his hand. Let's take a look at how you can create some veins.

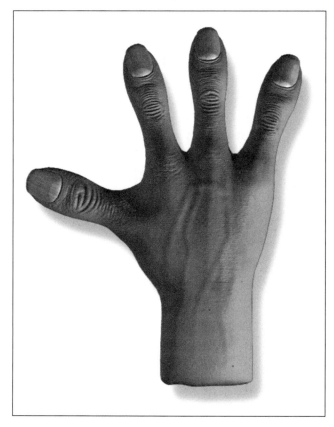

Figure 9.41 Scratch.

Realistic Veins

Veins can be an integral part of creating realism in any creature, especially if that creature consists only of a hand, like Scratch. Modeling veins can be very difficult and time consuming, but with a bump map they're pretty quick and easy to create. Let's get started.

Creating Veins

Note: *Be sure to write down the RGB values of the bump map's base color. This will come in handy when you are adding the other bump maps (for instance, when surfacing the front of the arm). Assigning all of the bump maps the same RGB base color ensures that seams won't appear between your bump image maps.*

1. Refer to some good reference images of hands. This reference imagery can be as close as the end of your arm. Your own hands tell you just where the veins pop up, where they begin and end, and how they meander under the surface of the skin. Figure 9.42 shows one of the reference images used to create the veins for Scratch.

2. To create a realistic vein bump map, you need to open the template image of the top of Scratch's hand, tophand.psd, in chapt9\Scratch on the companion CD-ROM.

3. Create a new layer called Bump.

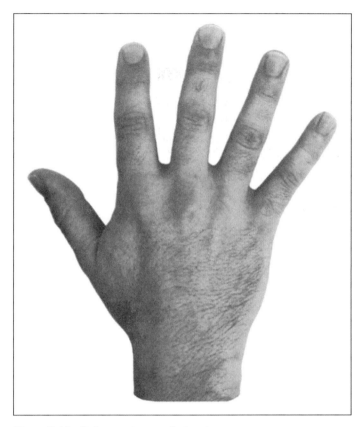

Figure 9.42   Reference image of a hand.

4. Select a dark gray color RGB 102, 102, 102 and fill the bump layer. This is the base color for the bump map.

5. Click on the foreground color and change it to white RGB 255, 255, 255. Double-click on the airbrush tool and give it the following settings:

   - Pressure: 15%
   - Diameter: 13 pixels
   - Hardness: 5%
   - Spacing: 5%
   - Default Roundness and Angle

6. Begin painting the veins at the top of the hand, as shown in Figure 9.43.

7. You may need to smudge the beginning and ending portions of the veins, because veins don't just pop up out of nowhere–they gradually protrude up from under the skin. Using the Smudge

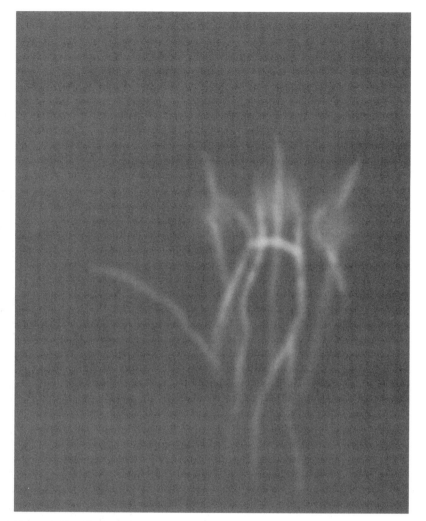

Figure 9.43 The bump map for Scratch's veins.

tool with the same airbrush settings used to paint the veins on and a pressure setting of 64%, smudge the ends of the veins. You may want to enhance the realism of the veins a bit by creating specularity and diffusion maps for them also, but that is just a simple matter of duplicating the bump map layer and tweaking the Brightness/Contrast. If you take another look in the Scratch folder, you should see another Photoshop file called Vein2.psd. This file contains the finished bump map along with the specularity and diffusion maps for the top of Scratch's hand.

If you take a look at Figure 9.41, you see the final result of your efforts—after planar-mapping the vein maps onto Scratch's hand. Now, let's take a look at another side of Scratch—his palm (see Figure 9.44).

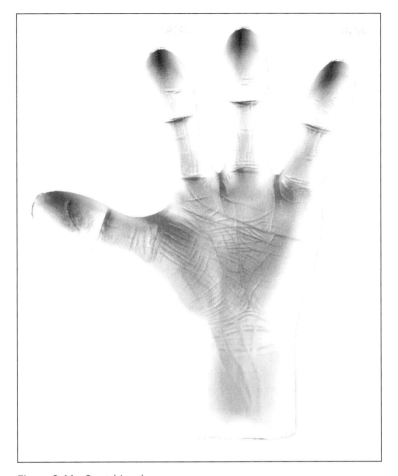

Figure 9.44   Scratch's palm.

Notice that Scratch has a pretty nasty cut on his thumb. This cut was caused one night while Scratch was pursuing one of his favorite past times: bowling. Let's take a look at how to create a scar like the one on Scratch's thumb.

Scars

Scars can really enhance a character's photorealistic credibility. They can help a character or creature look as if they've come into some harsh contact with your own physical world. Let's begin by loading the file called Scratchscar.psd from chapt9\Scratch on the companion CD-ROM.

Creating The Scar Bump Map

1. Create a new layer named Bump.

2. Fill the layer with the base bump color RGB 103,103, 103.

3. Hit the D key on the keyboard to set the colors to default (black in the foreground and white in the background) and select the black color RGB 0, 0, 0.

4. Double-click on the airbrush icon and give it the following settings:
   - Pressure: 83%
   - Normal
   - Diameter: 4 pixels
   - Hardness: 79%
   - Spacing: 25%
   - Default Angle and Roundness

   Using this airbrush, create a dark line or slash to represent the cut. Be sure to set the bump map's opacity to about 64% so you can see the template below. Don't go outside the confines of the templates boundaries (represented as the red color of the thumb render).

5. Set the Smudge tool to the following settings:
   - Pressure: 30%
   - Normal
   - Diameter: 13 pixels
   - Hardness: 5%
   - Spacing: 5%
   - Default Angle and Roundness

   Using the Smudge tool, taper the extreme edges of the black cut mark that you just painted (see Figure 9.45).

6. Using a combination of the Burn and Dodge tools, add details to the bump map until it looks similar to Figure 9.46. This is the completed bump map for Scratch's thumb.

Figure 9.45 The tapered cut on Scratch's thumb.

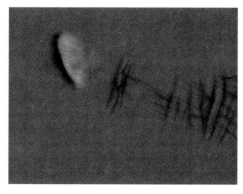

Figure 9.46 The completed bump map for Scratch's scar.

Now that you have the bump map for the scar, you're ready to add some color.

Adding Color To The Scar

1. To add some color to the scar, create a new layer named Color.

2. Choose Select All and fill the layer with a base skin tone RGB 252, 169, 130.

3. Create a new reddish color RGB 213, 102, 91 and create a new airbrush with the following settings:
   - Pressure: 5%
   - Normal
   - Diameter: 36 pixels
   - Hardness: 18%
   - Spacing: 25%
   - Default Angle and Roundness

4. Using this new airbrush, paint an area around the cut to create an inflamed look. Make sure that the color layer's opacity is set to around 64% so that you can see where the cut is on the bump map layer beneath it.

5. Create a deeper red color RGB 118, 39, 40 and a new airbrush with the following settings:
   - Pressure: 47%
   - Normal
   - Diameter: 5 pixels
   - Hardness: 10%
   - Spacing: 5%
   - Default Angle and Roundness

6. Paint the area directly over the cut to create the dried and clotted blood in the wound.

7. You can add a few touches with the Burn and Dodge tools to give the color map of the scar a little more variety (see Figure 9.47).

The final maps you need to create to complete Scratch's scar are the diffusion and specularity maps.

The Diffusion And Specularity Maps For Scratch's Scar

Open the file Scratchscar2.psd in the Scratch folder on the CD-ROM to view the specularity and diffusion maps for Scratch's scar. To create both the specularity and diffusion maps, I could have simply duplicated the bump map layer and adjusted the Brightness/Contrast. The only changes needed then would be to brighten the wound area for the specularity map (with the Dodge tool) and darken the wound area for the diffusion map (with the Burn tool).

Now, you have just one final detail to add to Scratch's skin surface—the bone and tendon bumps.

Bones And Tendons

Now that you've gotten your hands dirty (or, in this case, bloody), you need to enhance the look of Scratch's tendons and bones. To do this, create a good bump map to achieve the effect of protruding tendons and bones.

Creating Tendons And Bones With The Bump Map

Open the Scratchtendon.psd Photoshop file in chapt9\Scratch. In this image, you can see both the wireframe and the render templates for the back of Scratch's hand.

1. Create a new layer named Bump.

2. Select all of the bump map layer and fill it with a base gray color RGB 102, 102, 102.

3. Select the Dodge tool and give it the following settings:
   - Exposure: 14%
   - Midtones
   - Diameter: 36 pixels
   - Hardness: 18%
   - Spacing: 25%
   - Default Angle and Roundness

4. Remember to give the bump map layer an opacity setting of 64% so that you can see the render template beneath it. Using the Dodge tool, create several passes over the areas where the tendons and bones of the hand are (use your own hand for reference).

5. Set the layer's opacity back to 100% once the tendons are complete and use the Dodge tool to add any necessary touch ups. Figure 9.48 shows the final bump map for Scratch's tendons and bones.

Now let's give him the features that gave him his name: the fingernails.

Fingernail Textures

Although fingernails may look very similar to the skin at first glance, they're not. The surface of the fingernail is harder, shinier, and much less flexible. So, how can you add this look to the fingernails? Begin by adding their texture by bump mapping them.

Creating The Fingernail Bump Map

1. Open the Scratchnails.psd file, which is in chapt9\Scratch on the CD-ROM.

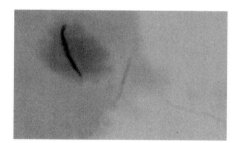

Figure 9.47 The completed color map for Scratch's scar.

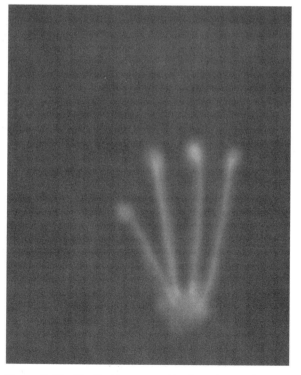

Figure 9.48 The final bump map for Scratch's tendons and bones.

2. Create the bump map layer. Name it Bump and set its opacity to 50%.

3. Using Photoshop's Square Selection tool, select an area that covers more than the entire area of the nail on the middle finger.

4. Return the layer's opacity to 100%.

5. Fill the selected area on the layer with white RGB 255, 255, 255.

6. Select Filter|Noise|Add Noise. Set the Noise filter to the following settings:
   - Amount: 56
   - Distribution: Gaussian
   - Check the Monochromatic box

7. Select Filter|Blur|Motion Blur and give it the following settings:
   - Angle: 90°
   - Distance
   - 15 pixels

   Apply this filter with the same settings two more times.

8. Select Image|Adjust|Brightness/Contrast and apply these settings: Brightness: -36, Contrast: +43. See Figure 9.49 for an example of how the selection area of your bump map layer should look at this point.

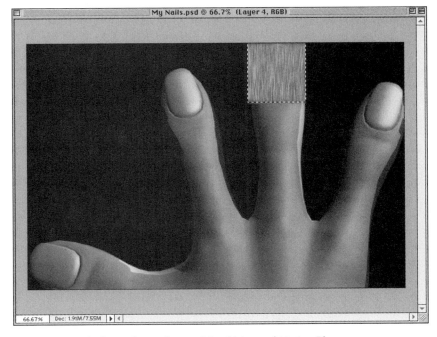

Figure 9.49 The bump layer after applying Noise and Motion Blur.

9. Make a copy of this selection and paste it into another layer.

10. Using Layer|Transform|Rotate, rotate and move the selection until it completely covers the fingernail for the index finger.

11. Repeat this procedure until you've covered each of the fingernails and thumbnails with the selection area you created.

12. When all of the fingernails have been covered with this bump map texture, link all of the bump map layers that you created and select Merge Linked from the layers palette.

That's it for the bump map layer. Now, you need to move on to creating the specularity layer. This is a good time to save your work if you haven't already.

Creating The Specularity Map For The Fingernails

1. Duplicate the bump map layer that you just created and name it Specularity.

2. Select Brightness/Contrast and apply these settings: Brightness: -40, Contrast: +18.

That's all you need to do to create the specularity. All you need now is the diffusion map and lucky for you, the image that you created for the bump map will work fine as a diffusion map. Simply duplicate the bump map layer and name it Diffusion. Save this Photoshop file and save each of the maps as a separate image. Your final task now is to create the color map for Scratch's fingernails.

Creating The Color Map For The Fingernails

1. Create a new layer named Color.

2. Create a skin color RGB 250, 169, 136.

3. Create a new paint brush and give it these brush settings:
   - Opacity: 100%
   - Normal
   - Diameter: 78 pixels
   - Hardness: 100%
   - Spacing: 25%
   - Default Angle and Roundness

4. Change the color layer's opacity to 64% so that you can see the rendered template beneath it.

5. Liberally paint the flesh color over the white nails until each one is covered.

6. Using your own hand as reference, add the color changes to the nail. Be sure to get the little details, like dirt beneath the fingernails and the near-white moons where the nail attaches to the finger. Figure 9.50 shows the final color map for scratch's fingernails.

Take a look at what the combination of texture mapped bones, tendons, veins, pores, and wrinkle maps does to provide photorealistic quality to your 3D models (see Figure 9.51).

Another way that you can enhance your model's realism is by using bump maps to help define the creature's muscles. Let's take a look at a character that uses a muscle bump map.

Getting To Know Pawn

Pawn is actually the little brother of Spawn. He's a comical takeoff on Todd Mcfarlane's spectacular super hero. A stunted version of his big brother, he has all of Spawn's accessories, he just doesn't use them as well. Pawn can be found tripping over his cape while attempting to fight the villains of the world. Figure 9.52 shows Pawn.

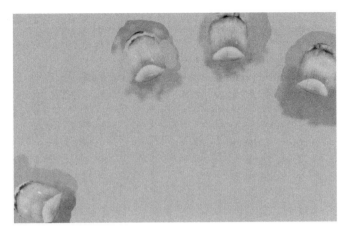

Figure 9.50 The final fingernail color map.

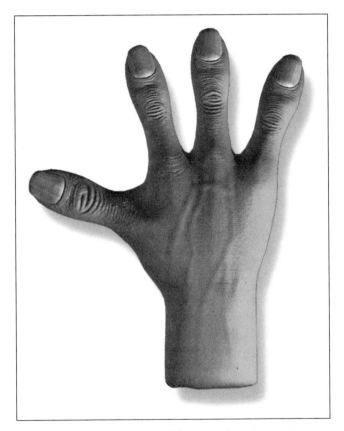

Figure 9.51 The final render of the top of Scratch's hand.

Figure 9.52   Pawn.

To create Pawn's protective suit, which is covered with striated muscles, you'll need to use extensive bump mapping.

Muscle Bump Maps

In order to create Pawn's muscle bump map, you need to open the Pawnmuscle.psd Photoshop file in chapt9\Pawn. This is the front shot of Pawn that you'll be planar-mapping the bump map to. Reference images of Spawn abound, so just pick one of the *Spawn* magazines to see where to create the muscles.

Creating Muscle Bump Maps

1. Create a new layer named Bump. Fill the layer with the base gray color RGB 111, 111, 111.

2. Select the Burn tool and begin painting the muscle striations onto Pawn with the following Burn tool settings:

    - Exposure: 32%

    - Midtones

    - Diameter: 4 pixels

    - Hardness: 79%

    - Spacing: 25%

    - Default Angle and Roundness

3. After the striations have been painted, select the Dodge tool, using the same brush size and exposure settings as above. Lighten the areas between the dark striations, as shown in Figure 9.53.

4. Utilize the Burn and Dodge tools to finish painting Pawn's muscles, changing the brush diameter and exposure settings as needed. Figure 9.54 shows the final results of using only the Burn and Dodge tools to create the muscle bump map.

Pawn still needs a few more texture maps before he's ready to do battle with all those minions from hell. So, let's give him that great slimy look that movie creatures seem to like so much.

Creating That Slimy Look For Your Creature

The best way to give a creature the slimy look is with a combination of specularity and diffusion mapping. Let's create these image maps for Pawn.

Creating The Slimy Specularity Map

1. Duplicate the bump map for the muscles you just made and name it Specularity.

2. Open Brightness/Contrast Set the Brightness to +31 and the Contrast to +23.

3. Copy the specularity layer and save it as a new file onto your hard drive, naming it Pawnspec.

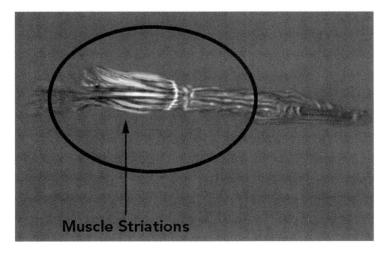

Muscle Striations

Figure 9.53 The striations in Pawn's muscle maps.

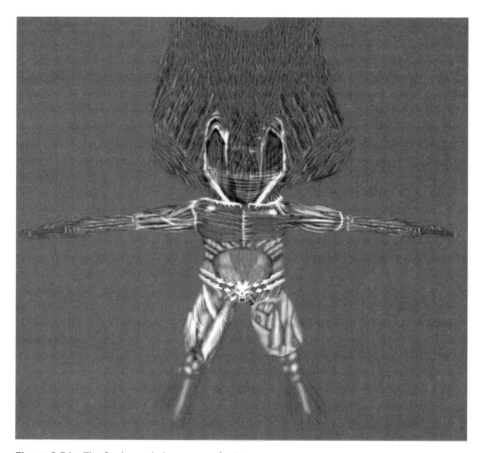

Figure 9.54   The final muscle bump map for Pawn.

Creating The Slimy Diffusion Map

1. Duplicate the bump map again and name it Diffusion.

2. Open Brightness/Contrast Set the Brightness to -20 and the Contrast to -84.

3. Copy and save the diffusion layer as Pawndiff.

4. Planar-map the bump, specularity, and diffusion maps onto the Pawn model in the Pawn folder.

   Be sure to map the images along the Z axis, so that they stick to the front of Pawn. Figure 9.55 shows the end result of your efforts after applying the bump, diffusion, and specularity maps that you just created. This figure has an added color map to finish the effect.

Pawn is definitely a slimy, muscular superhero. You can see how these relatively simple image maps have transformed a simple cartoon character into a menacing superhero.

Figure 9.55 The final Pawn.

Moving On

I'm sure you've noticed that many of the techniques used to surface a character or creature are very similar. Whether you're surfacing Gorg's lizard head or Dr. Dread's teeth, the same methods are employed again and again—such as copying layers and manipulating them to create a completely new image map for the surface of a character and utilizing strong visual reference material to get an idea of what you're trying to paint really looks like. These technical aspects of 3D surfacing can be taught, but it takes your own creative approach and imagination to really raise the bar in the world of art and 3D graphics.

PAINTING CHARACTER
ACCESSORIES 10

Most 3D artists spend a lot of time working on the face of their character, which is great, but not if the face is attached to a shiny bald head and a body with clothes that look as if they were made by Fisher-Price.

Accessories are an important part of any believable 3D creature or character. By accessories I mean those often overlooked additions, such as clothing, hair, or fur. We'll start with creating realistic clothing.

Creating Realistic Clothing

If you want your 3D characters to come across as real, it helps to dress them in realistic clothing. The steps for creating such clothing are:

- Creating the cloth pattern as a color map.

- Adding stains to the color map.

- Creating the thread texture for the cloth as a bump map.

- Adding wrinkles to the shirt with bump mapping.

- Adding sweat stains to the shirt with a diffusion map.

You'll start by making the color pattern for the cloth.

The Color For Dr. Dread's Shirt

Do you remember Dr. Dread from the last chapter? Well, you're going to get him dressed in this chapter. Although you'll be working only on a portion of Dr. Dread's shirt for this tutorial, the concepts covered here can be used for any type of clothing.

Once again, it's necessary to find some good visual-reference material to help guide the process. I just pulled one of my old shirts off the rack and hung it up next to my monitor. You could do the same. Once you've got your reference material secured, you can get started on the following project.

Creating Cloth Texture

1. Create a 41×41 pixel file.

2. Choose Select All and fill this layer for the shirt with an off-white base color, RGB 247, 239, 236.

3. Create a new blue-gray color, RGB 114, 121, 126.

4. Select the Line tool and set the options to:

   - Normal

   - Opacity: 100%

   - Line Width: 4 pixels

   - Anti-aliased

5. Holding down the Shift key on your keyboard (this keeps the line perfectly straight), create a vertical line on the far left side of the image that reaches from the top to the bottom.

6. Create another line—a horizontal one—stretching from the top left to the top right of the image as shown in Figure 10.1.

7. Create a new reddish-brown color, RGB 153, 114, 119.

8. Select the Line tool again and change the width to 2 pixels, leaving all the other Line tool settings as they were.

9. Hold down the Shift key to create a horizontal line about 13 pixels down from the top of image.

10. Using this same reddish-brown color, change the line width to 1 pixel and set the Opacity to 85%.

11. Create two thin lines with the Line tool: one horizontally just above the thick reddish-brown line you created and one vertically on the far right side. Remember to hold the Shift key down when making each of these lines (see Figure 10.2).

Now, you need to test this swatch of cloth color to see if it works as a seamlessly tileable image for Dr. Dread's shirt. Complete the steps to test your color.

Testing The Color Pattern For Tileability

1. Select the entire color map image.

2. Choose Edit|Define Pattern.

3. Create an 82×82 pixel file.

4. Select All of this new file.

5. Select Edit|Fill|Contents: Use Pattern. The resulting image is shown in Figure 10.3.

Figure 10.1 The first two lines for Dr. Dread's shirt.

Figure 10.2 The pattern for Dr. Dread's shirt.

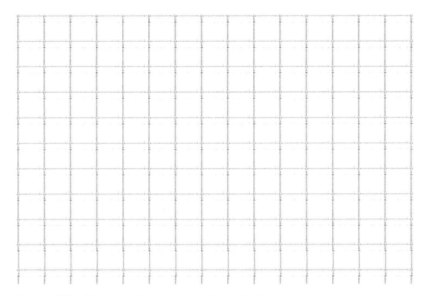

Figure 10.3 The tiled color map for Dr. Dread's shirt.

That looks pretty good. Now, use this pattern to map the surface to Dr. Dread's shirt, following the steps in the next project.

Painting Dr. Dread's Shirt

1. Open the Dreadshirt.psd file located in the Chapter 10\Dr_Dread folder on the companion CD-ROM. This file contains the template for Dr. Dread's shirt, as shown in Figure 10.4.

2. Create a new layer named Color.

3. Because you still have the color pattern for the shirt in Photoshop's pattern memory, you just need to select all of the color layer and fill it with the pattern at 100% Opacity.

4. Make a copy of the color layer and save it as a separate file that can be read by your 3D program.

To apply the image map to Dread's shirt, load the Dread_Shirt object file from chapt10\Dr_Dread on the companion CD-ROM into your 3D program. Now, you have a seamless cloth pattern covering the entire image, as shown in Figure 10.5.

With the cloth pattern covering the template of Dr. Dread's shirt, you can now add some stains and dirt to the shirt to make it more believable. Perfectly clean shirts do exist, but they certainly lack a story. Every element we surface has a story. The shirt has been many places and experienced many things. Since Dr. Dread is so highly focused on

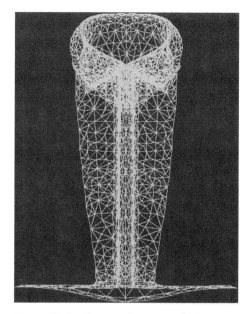

Figure 10.4   The template image for Dr. Dread's shirt.

Figure 10.5   The cloth pattern covering Dr. Dread's shirt.

his work, he rarely has time to concern himself with being neat. Therefore, you can assume he's got some stains on his clothing. Let's dirty up Dr. Dread's shirt.

Stains On Clothing

Because Dr. Dread loves to munch on cheeseburgers while working those late hours, he tends to drip a lot of catsup and mustard onto his shirt. To top it off, being a maniacal worker, he sweats a lot and rarely gets to the Laundromat. Put that together with a very dirty laboratory and you can see how Dr. Dread's shirt would look a little lived in, to say the least. To surface Dr. Dread's shirt, start by creating some colors for the stains.

The following project illustrates a quick method for creating color palettes.

Creating A Color Stain Palette

1.   Create a new 150×100 pixel file.

2.   Create a red catsup stain color, RGB 61, 13, 11, and paint this color onto the image using a paintbrush with 100% Opacity. Do the same for the mustard color, RGB 168, 112, 43, and the dirt color, RGB 35, 24, 17. The swatch palette should look similar to Figure 10.6.

3.   Select an airbrush with these settings:

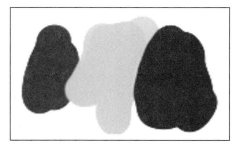

Figure 10.6 Swatch for the stains on Dr. Dread's shirt (see figure in Color Studio).

- Normal

- Pressure: 12%

- Diameter: 36 pixels

- Hardness: 18%

- Spacing: 25%

- Default Angle and Roundness

4. Move the color swatch so that it's easily accessible beside the Dreadshirt.psd file.

5. Make sure that you're in the Color layer of the Dreadshirt.psd file and test out the catsup color by holding down the mouse button only once, so that you can Undo the test.

6. When you're happy with the settings, Undo the test and set the color layer's Opacity to 50% so you can see the template beneath the Color layer.

7. Paint the catsup stains onto Dr. Dread's shirt, using the template as a guide. Place the stains where you think the stains would occur, such as those shown in Figure 10.7.

8. Using the airbrush (with the same settings), select the mustard color on the color swatch file by holding down the Option key (Mac) or Alt key (Windows). This temporarily turns the airbrush into the Eyedropper tool.

9. Move back to the Color layer for Dr. Dread's shirt and add the mustard and dirt colors to the shirt, using the same steps you did for the catsup stains.

Now that you've stained the color pattern, you need to do one more thing to make the planar mapping more realistic. If you were to planar map the shirt pattern right now, Dr. Dread's shirt would look like Figure 10.8.

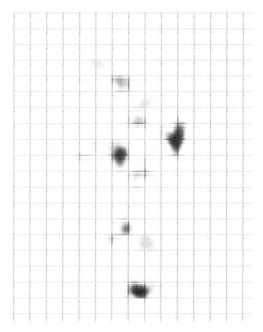

Figure 10.7 Painting the catsup stains on Dr. Dread's shirt (see figure in Color Studio).

Figure 10.8 Your shirt pattern is almost there.

Did you notice that there is something a little strange about the collar? The problem is that the shirt collar pattern exactly matches the rest of the cloth pattern. This would not happen in reality because the shirt collar would be folded back. What you need to do is fold the collar area in the image map so that it matches the actual collar fold of the shirt.

Folding Back The Shirt Collar

1. Give the color layer an Opacity setting of 40%. This will make the template layers beneath it visible. Start out using the rendered template layer for reference, but refer to the wireframe for the actual selection because the wireframe is a more accurate representation of what the image will map to.

2. Select the Lasso tool. Hold down the Option key (Mac) or Alt key (Windows) and select the front of the collar area. Holding down the Option (or Alt) key allows you to make one mouse click to connect straight lines. See Figure 10.9.

3. After you've selected and saved the selection for the left collar, do the same for the right collar.

4. Using the square selection tool, make a selection of the color map pattern, as shown in Figure 10.10.

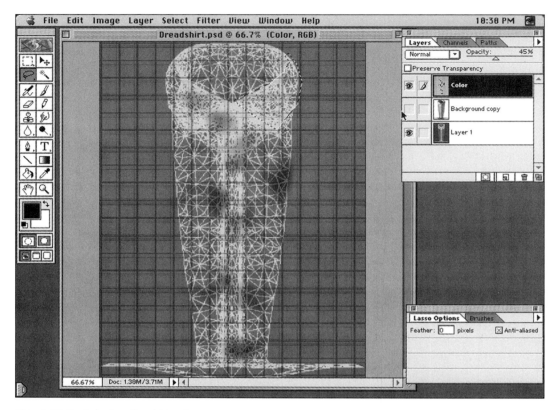

Figure 10.9 Selecting the shirt collar.

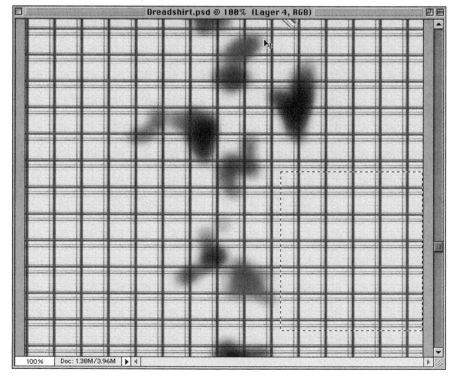

Figure 10.10 Creating a selection of the color map.

5. Make a copy of this selection and paste it into a new layer.

6. Select Layer|Transform|Numeric and rotate the image 45 degrees.

7. Move the rotated layer over to where the right collar is located.

8. Choose Select|Load Selection and load the selection you saved for the right collar.

9. Be sure that you're in the rotated selections layer and make a copy of the rotated image, as shown in Figure 10.11.

10. Make a copy of the rotated section using the selection of the collar that you just loaded.

11. Paste this collar section into a new layer. Then, do the same for the left side of the collar. The results should look like Figure 10.12.

12. Select the first color layer that you created and the two shirt-collar layers.

13. Link the shirt-collar layers to the original color layer and select Merge Linked.

14. Make a copy of the composite color layer and save it as a separate file that can be read by your 3D program.

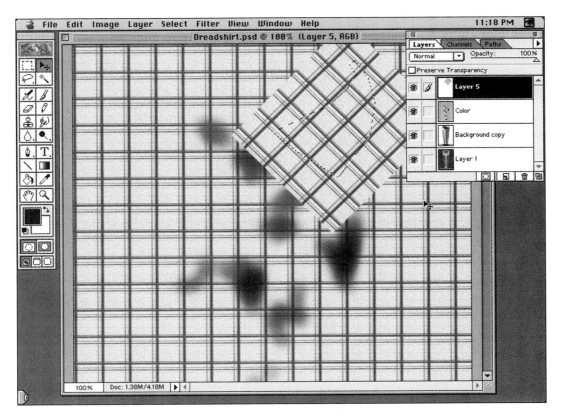

Figure 10.11   Copying the rotated collar.

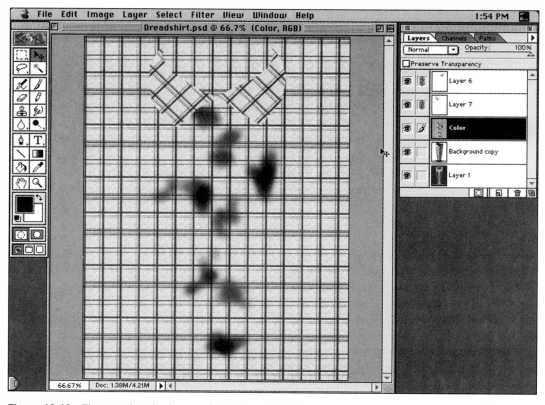

Figure 10.12 The completed color map for Dr. Dread's shirt.

That completes the color map for Dr. Dread's shirt, but you still need to give the shirt some texture.

Thread Texture For Fabric

You have several options for creating a realistic thread texture for Dr. Dread's shirt. If you have a scanner, you could simply grab a linen sheet off your bed and scan it. If you don't have a scanner, you could paint the thread texture, but that could take a long time. Fortunately, you're using Photoshop, which has a pretty good cloth texture filter. You need to create a seamless, tileable texture for the cloth pattern, so let's get started by creating the thread texture.

Creating Thread Texture

1. Create a new file that is 100×75 pixels. Be sure that the white color swatch is behind the black, so that the image is white when you create this new file.

2. Select Filter|Texture|Texturizer and apply these settings:

   • Texture: Canvas

   • Scaling: 50%

- Relief: 8

- Light Direction: Top Right

3. Test this cloth pattern to see if it's both seamless and tileable. First, choose Select All and define it as a pattern. Then, create a new file that is 200×300 pixels. The results should look like Figure 10.13.

4. If your 3D program allows you to apply multiple bump maps to objects, save the cloth texture bump map as a separate file and name it Dreadshirtbump1.

Most 3D programs can support only a single image map layer, so you'll need to perform a few additional steps to add a few details to the bump map for Dr. Dread's shirt. Typically, these details are added as separate bump map layers, so you have more precise control over their effect.

Creating Thread Texture For Single Layer Systems

1. Open Dreadshirt.psd if it's not open already.

2. Create a new layer named Bump.

3. Select the Dreadshirtbump1 file and select the Brightness/Contrast control.

4. Reduce the Brightness to -80, and reduce the contrast to -43.

5. Choose Select All and define this as a pattern.

6. Go back to the Bump layer in our Dreadshirt.psd file and fill it with this pattern. The results should look like Figure 10.14.

Figure 10.13 The cloth texture bump map.

Figure 10.14 The cloth texture bump map layer.

Now, you're ready to combine bump map layers. You'll be creating more bump layers in just a moment. So for now, simply save the file.

Dr. Dread's shirt looks much more natural now that you've added a nice color pattern and texture to the cloth, but there's still something not quite right about this shirt. There aren't any wrinkles!

Wrinkles On Dr. Dread's Shirt

Dr. Dread's shirt looks as if it were starched and pressed until it hurts. Even a freshly ironed shirt has some wrinkles, but a shirt that hasn't been changed for three days—like Dr. Dread's—has more than its fair share. Complete the following project to add some wrinkles.

Creating Fabric Wrinkles

1. Open the Dreadshirt.psd file and select the Bump layer.

2. Select the Burn tool with these settings:

    *   Exposure: 35%

    *   Diameter: 13 pixels

    *   Hardness: 5%

    *   Spacing: 5%

    *   Default Angle and Roundness

3. After testing the Burn tool's settings and undoing the results, set the Opacity for the Bump layer to 50%.

4. Referring frequently to your shirt model, use the Burn tool to match the wrinkle indentations on the shirt. Be sure to emulate the stitch areas around the collar and where the shirt connects in the center. You'll need to change the Burn tool's brush diameter settings frequently and touch up the wrinkles with the Dodge tool before you're finished. Take a look at Figure 10.15 to see what the final bump map should look like.

5. Copy the Bump map layer and save it in a file format that your 3D program can read. Also, save the Dreadshirt.psd file.

That does it for the fabric bump textures. Now, let's add some sweat stains to the shirt.

Sweat Stains For Dr. Dread's Shirt

The final step in creating photorealistic cloth is adding Diffusion and Specularity maps to the model. You'll start with the Diffusion map.

Creating The Fabric Diffusion Map

1. Duplicate the Bump layer of the Dreadshirt.psd file and name this layer Diffusion.

2. Open the Brightness/Contrast dialog box and set the Brightness to +88 and the Contrast to -54.

Because Dr. Dread has been working so many hours in the lab, he would have quite a few sweat stains covering his shirt, so let's add some.

Adding Sweat Stains To Fabric

1. Be sure that you're in the Diffusion layer and set its Opacity to 75%.

2. Hit the D key to select the Default colors.

3. Select a Paintbrush with these settings:

    *   Opacity: 8%

    *   Diameter: 24 pixels

    *   Hardness: 100%

    *   Spacing: 4%

    *   Default Angle and Roundness

4. Using the paintbrush with the black color, paint the sweat stains around Dr. Dread's collar and chest area.

5. Change the diameter of the paintbrush to 6 pixels and paint over the edges of the sweat stains to create the effect shown in Figure 10.16.

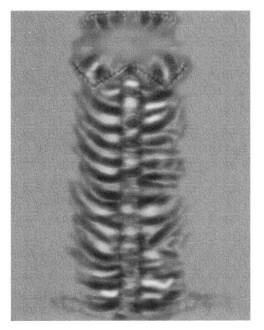

Figure 10.15   The final bump map for Dr. Dread's shirt.

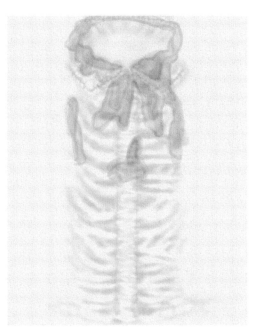

Figure 10.16   Painting the sweat stains onto the Diffusion map.

6. Copy the Diffusion layer and save it in a file format that your 3D program can read. Be sure to save your Dreadshirt.psd file as well.

7. Switch to your 3D program and planar map the Color, Bump, and Diffusion maps along the Z axis (unless Z is up and down in your program) onto the 3D object of Dr. Dread's shirt. The results should look like Figure 10.17.

Cloth is often overlooked as one of the necessary details to a character's overall realism, but the one detail that is most overlooked is hair.

Figure 10.17   The final render of Dr. Dread's shirt.

Creating Realistic Hair

I don't think that there's a larger population of bald or bathing-cap-wearing characters than in the world of 3D graphics. Why so many bald 3D characters? Because hair is hard to create with 3D tools! Some 3D programs have addressed the shortcomings of creating hair with particle systems or special fur shaders, but these solutions are mainly found in the higher-end, wallet-intensive programs. If you're in the low to midrange category, you can create some pretty incredible hair by using simple image mapping techniques.

To create realistic hair for a 3D character, you first need to have a head to work with. For this purpose, you'll be adding a full head of hair to Charlie, the incomparable accountant. Charlie's lost an awful lot of hair sweating over those IRS audits through the years, but you, as a generous 3D artist, can replace it (even without the aid of miracle cures).

In this section, you'll be learning the following steps for creating realistic hair:

- Creating a seamless, tileable color map of the hair.

- Creating hair bump maps.

- Adding specularity to the hair.

- Creating clip maps for the hair.

Color Maps For Charlie's Hair

There are a couple of effective ways to create realistic hair image maps. One of the best methods I've found is to take a wig and scan it. If you do not have a scanner, you can use Photoshop's tools to create the hair images. I've also provided a scanned image of a wig, which can be found in chapt10\Charlie on the companion CD. The file is called Charliewig.psd.

Let's create some hair for Charlie.

Creating Hair Color Maps

1. Create a new 500×500 pixel file and name it Charliehair.psd.

2. Name the background layer Color.

3. Change the color in the foreground layer to the hair color that you want for Charlie. I chose a dark brown, RGB 34, 14, 4.

4. Choose Select All and fill the color layer with this color.

5. Create a new layer and leave its name as is (layer 1).

6. Change the foreground to a darker brown, RGB 11, 1, 1, and fill this new layer (layer 1) with the color.

7. Click on the layer mask button, which can be found at the bottom of the Layers panel. The layer mask mode makes it possible to paint with black to reveal the layer below and to paint with white to hide it.

8. Set the colors to default (white in foreground).

9. Choose Filter|Render|Clouds. The results should match Figure 10.18.

10. Select the Filter|Difference Clouds and apply five times.

11. Select Filter|Stylize|Find Edges.

12. Choose Image|Adjust Levels and give it Input Levels 161, 0.24, 255 and Output Levels 0, 255. The image should begin to look a little bit like hair, as shown in Figure 10.19.

13. Select a little less than half of the bottom portion using the Square Selection tool, as shown in Figure 10.20.

14. Choose Select|Transform Selection (or Layer| Free Transform, if you're using Photoshop 4), select the top center handle and stretch the

Figure 10.18 The hair color map after applying the cloud filter.

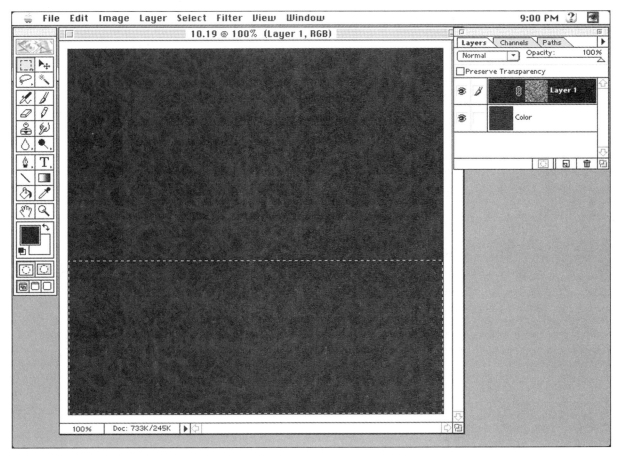

Figure 10.19 The hair after adjusting the levels.

Figure 10.20   Selecting the bottom portion of the image.

selection to the top of the canvas. Double-click in the center of the selected area and then drop the selection. The results of this operation should match Figure 10.21.

15. Select Brightness/Contrast and increase the Contrast to +27.

16. Flatten the image and select Image|Rotate Canvas 90 degrees CW.

17. Select the Dodge tool with an Exposure of 50% and the following paintbrush settings:

  • Diameter: 3 pixels

  • Hardness: 100%

  • Spacing: 25%

  • Default Angle and Roundness

18. Create horizontal marks across the image to represent strands of hair (avoiding the top and bottom edges of the image), as shown in Figure 10.22.

19. You need to apply a few filters to finish the color map. Choose Filter|Stylize|Wind, select the Blast radio button under the Method section, and select From the Left radio button under the Direction section.

20. Select Filter|Blur|Motion Blur, Angle 0, and a Distance of 5 pixels.

21. Select Filter|Sharpen|Sharpen to finish the hair color, as shown in Figure 10.23.

Figure 10.21 The stretched image of the hair.

Figure 10.22 Creating strands of hair with the Dodge tool.

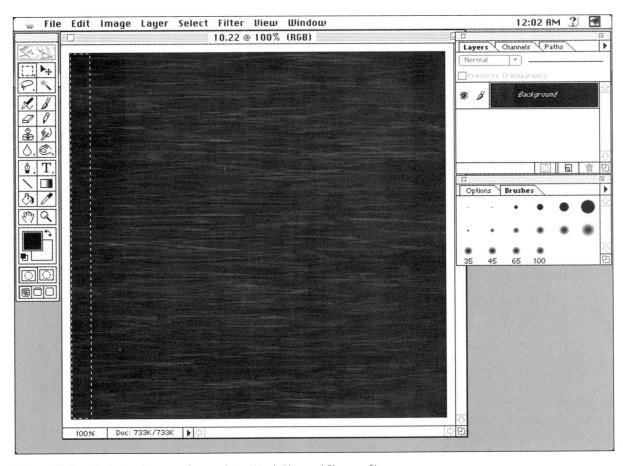

Figure 10.23 The hair color map after applying Wind, Blur, and Sharpen filters.

Now that you have the basic hair color, you need to make the hair color map seamless and tileable.

Making The Hair Color Map Seamless And Tileable

1. Make a selection from the far-left side of the image and about 27 pixels in toward the center, as shown in Figure 10.24.

2. Copy the selection and paste it into a new layer.

3. Choose Layer|Transform|Flip Horizontal.

4. With the Move tool, hold down the Shift key and slide this new layer all the way to the far right of the image. You may need to use the arrow keys on the keyboard to get the layer to exactly match up with the far right edge.

5. Select the Eraser tool and give it the following settings:

   • Opacity: 75%

   • Diameter: 3 pixels

   • Hardness: 100%

   • Spacing: 25%

   • Default Angle and Roundness

   Erase the outer left edge of the new layer until the edge is no longer visible and no difference can be distinguished between the top and bottom layers.

6. Flatten the image.

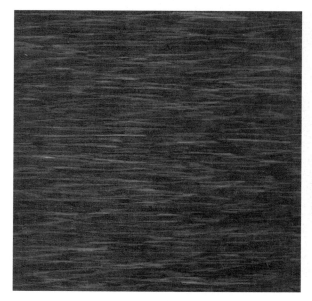

Figure 10.24   The far left selection.

The color map should now be both seamless and tileable. To test it, follow the three steps in the "Testing The Color Pattern For Tileability" project at the beginning of this chapter.

(If you are using the file of the scanned wig for the color map—Charliewig.psd—the following steps apply for creating the bump, specularity and clip maps.)

Now that you've created a good, tileable, color map for the hair, you need to add the hair texture.

Bump Maps For Hair Texture

Adding texture begins with making a bump map.

Creating The Hair Texture

1. Duplicate the Color layer and name it Bump.

2. Select Image|Adjust|Hue/Saturation and turn the Saturation all the way down to -100.

3. With the Brightness/Contrast Control, set the Contrast to +70.

4. Choose the Filter|Blur|Gaussian Blur and set the Radius to 0.3 pixels. This softens the abruptness of the hair's texture. The bump map for Charlie's hair should look like Figure 10.25.

Specularity: Give It Some Shine

It was easy enough to create the hair's texture. Now, you just need to add the shine or *specularity* to the hair.

Figure 10.25 The bump map for Charlie's hair.

Adding Shine To Hair

1. Duplicate the Bump layer and name the new layer Specularity.

2. Using Brightness/Contrast, set the Brightness to -12 and the Contrast to -59. With the Brightness setting, you'll be able to make the hair shinier by increasing the value, and vice versa. Take a look at Figure 10.26 to see what the final specularity map should look like.

Clip Maps

At last, you've come to the final image map for Charlie's hair, the clip map. Some 3D programs don't give you the option to create clip maps, but the steps laid out here also work for transparency maps. The difference between the two is that clip maps make portions of the object either visible or invisible, whereas transparency maps read grays as semitransparent.

Typically, white is opaque and black is transparent for clip maps. That means that wherever you see black in the hair clip map, you'll see through the hair to the skin color of Charlie's skull.

If you can, use a clip map for the hair because not many people have semitransparent hair.

Creating The Hair Clip Map

1. Make a duplicate of the Bump layer and name it Clip.

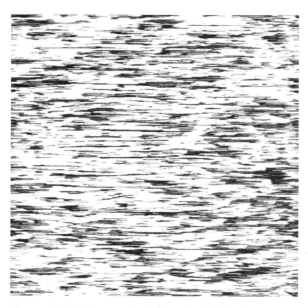

Figure 10.26   The specularity map for Charlie's hair.

2. Select Image|Adjust|Levels. Make sure that the Channels box is set to RGB and set the input levels to 0, 1, and 15. This should give you a good clip map that allows some portions of the skin below to show through the map.

Note: *If you want hair to appear thicker yet retain its volume, make the skin surface below the hair geometry a dark brown color, such as RGB 12, 2, 2.*

Saving The Layers And Applying Them To Charlie's Head

Now that you've created all of the maps for Charlie's hair, you just need to save each of the layers as a separate image and name them appropriately. Start with the color layer.

Saving Each Layer As A Separate Image

1. Select the entire Color layer.

2. Copy the selected layer and create a new file.

3. Paste the Color image from the Clipboard into the new file. Be sure to flatten the image.

4. Save the image as Haircolor in a file format that your 3D program can read.

5. Repeat this process for the rest of the image maps, naming them appropriately.

Now, you are ready to put the hair on Charlie's head.

Placing The Hair Maps Onto Charlie's Hair Geometry

1. Load each hair image map into your 3D program.

2. Open the Charliehead and Charliehair geometry files from the chapt10\Charlie\Objects directory on the CD-ROM and choose the file format that your 3D program can read.

3. Planar-map each of the image maps onto the Charliehair object along the Y axis. Be sure to keep the same tiling settings for each of the maps so that they all line up exactly with one another.

Figure 10.27 shows the final results of hair mapping using the scanned image of the wig.

Creating realistic hair gives you a pretty good argument for getting a scanner—not just for the time that it can save you, but also for the photorealism it can provide. If you pay close attention to the details of the natural world and endeavor to build your skills in reproducing those subtle details, you can create realism for even the most fantastical flights of imagination.

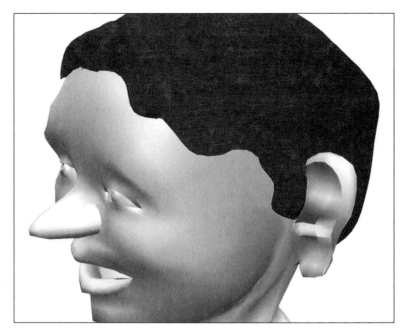

Figure 10.27 Charlie with the scanned image of the hair.

Moving On

There are literally thousands of potential character details. Unfortunately, we couldn't cover all of them in this chapter. When creating your characters, you need to focus the same amount of effort on surfacing the details as you did with the character's skin. It also helps to place your characters in realistic surroundings, which you'll learn about in the next chapter.

PAINTING NATURAL
TEXTURES 11

The only way to really convince the viewer that natural textures in a 3D scene are "real" is with texture maps. Although you may not study leaves, rocks, and blades of grass, you subconsciously know their texture. This is why when you see a 3D leaf with a green shader applied to it, it looks fake. From a distance the leaves may not appear fake, but up close their reality crumbles. This is why you must use texture maps.

Not so long ago, seeing realistic leaves, trees, bushes, and rocks was pretty rare in 3D. The reason is that 3D programs simply weren't sophisticated enough to allow artists to imbue the 3D landscapes with realism. Nowadays, that has all changed, and telling the actual, natural world from one constructed entirely in 3D is getting pretty difficult. Well, visually anyway.

One aspect that's imperative to creating photorealistic, natural scenes in 3D is creating believable image maps for your scenery. In this chapter we'll be covering the ins and outs of creating the image maps for the following natural textures:

- Dirt and sand color maps
- Dirt and sand bump maps
- Rock and mineral color maps
- Rock and mineral bump maps
- Leaves color maps
- Leaves bump maps

At this point, you can just jump right in and get started with creating some dirt and sand color maps.

Creating Sand And Dirt Color Maps

Unless you're a pretty morose individual, you probably don't spend an awful lot of time walking around staring at the ground, but if you want to create truly believable sand and dirt that looks as though you could walk around on it, you really should spend some time observing what real dirt looks like. Figure 11.1 shows some samples of sand and dirt that I've put together.

As you can see, you have quite a variety to choose from. You have such a choice because a wide range of conditions—moisture, lack of moisture, elevation, pH of the soil, and so on—influence the appearance of the earth. Something that you need to consider before embarking on the time-consuming process of creating color maps for the dirt is the mood of the scene you're creating. After all, you don't want to create all the image maps for the earth in a sunlit, midday, outdoor scene only to decide later that what would really suit the mood of the scene is a rainy, late-night atmosphere. So, as you can see, something as seemingly insignificant as the dirt in the scene can really prove to be of major importance when it comes to completing the scene in the most timely fashion possible.

Figure 11.1 Some samples of sand and dirt.

Say that you want your scene to take place at midday with a clear sky, with dry, sandy, and fairly hard-packed ground. Because the ground usually covers a large area of a scene, a good method for image-mapping the sand is to create a seamless, tileable image map. By doing so, you can create relatively small image maps for the sand and then reproduce them to cover the large surface of the ground.

Creating The Color Map For The Sand

To get started, follow these steps to create the color map for the sand:

1. Create a new file that's 300×300 pixels, and name it Sand.psd.

2. Create a base tone for the dirt, RGB 225, 195, 148.

3. Choose the Paint Bucket Tool, and fill the Background layer with the base color.

4. Select Filter|Noise|Add Noise. In the dialog box, set the Amount to 32, select Gaussian for the Distribution, and check the Monochromatic checkbox.

5. Add a little texture to the sand color by selecting Filter|Texture| Texturizer and giving it the following settings:

- Texture: Sandstone

- Scaling: 200%

- Relief: 5

- Light Direction: Top

The results should look like Figure 11.2 at this point.

6. To make sure that this image map is both seamless and tileable, you need to test it. Choose Select|All, and then select Edit|Define Pattern.

7. Select New|File, and create a file that's 600×600 pixels.

8. Select Edit|Fill; then select these settings—Contents: Use: Pattern. Be sure that the Opacity is set to 100% and the Mode is set to Normal. The results should look like Figure 11.3.

Fortunately, no visible seams are present in the tiled image. So, you're free to move on and create the bump map for the sand.

Creating The Sand Bump Map

To create the sand bump map, follow these steps:

1. Make a duplicate of the Background layer by choosing Duplicate Layer from the Layers palette, and name the new layer "Color". You can then delete the Background layer.

Figure 11.2 The final sand color map.

Figure 11.3 The seamless, tileable sand color map.

2. Now that you've freed the Color layer, make another duplicate of it, and name the duplicate "Bump".

3. With the Bump layer active, select Image|Adjust|Hue/Saturation.

4. In the dialog box, slide the Saturation slider all the way to the left (-100) so that all the color is removed from the layer. The Bump layer should resemble Figure 11.4 at this point.

5. Be sure to save the sand file that you just created as Sand.psd. Now, choose File|Save As, and save the file as Dirt.psd.

Now, you just need to save both the Color and Bump images in file formats that your 3D program can read. Map the image maps onto a flat 3D plane; adjust the specularity (low); and adjust the bump map amplitude (also low). Make sure to planar-map the image maps onto the plane, and keep the image tiling settings identical for both the Color and Bump map images. The results should resemble Figure 11.5.

As you can see, the plane looks a little barren all by itself. Also, getting a real feel for the size of the plane is pretty difficult without a person, rock, or road to judge its size against. I placed a common milk cow into the scene to help you get the perspective. Figure 11.6 shows the cow in its desolate surroundings.

Creating sand is straightforward, and because you've created the sand image maps, you can more easily transform the same image maps to create dirt or mud.

Figure 11.4 The completed bump map for the dirt.

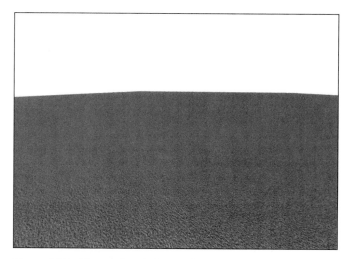

Figure 11.5 The rendered plane with the sand maps planar-mapped onto it.

Figure 11.6 The plane with a cow added to help with the perspective of the sand (see figure in Color Studio).

Creating Dirt Image Maps

To create the dirt image map, follow these steps:

1. Make the Color layer active.

2. Select Image|Adjust|Hue/Saturation , and set the Hue slider to +173, the Saturation to +36, and the Lightness to -71. These settings change the Color layer to something resembling Figure 11.7.

3. To create a little chaos in the dirt's color, select Filter|Distort|Ocean Ripple. Then, set Ripple Size to 3 and Ripple Magnitude to 4.

4. Because the result looks a little too bizarre for dirt at this point, select Filter|Texture|Craquelure. Then, set Crack Spacing to 15, Crack Depth to 0, and Crack Brightness to 2.

5. Boost the contrast so that the color differences stand out a bit more in the dirt. To do so, select Image|Adjust|Brightness/Contrast. In the dialog box, leave the Brightness at 0 and set the Contrast to +50.

6. The trouble now is that the blue in the dirt's color is too saturated, but you can fix that by selecting Image|Adjust|Hue/Saturation. In the dialog box, leave the Hue at O, lower the Saturation to -53, and set the Lightness to -21.

7. For the final touch, add a little more debris to the dirt by selecting Filter|Noise|Dust & Scratches. Here, set the Radius to 1 pixel and the Threshold to 125 levels.

You still need to make sure that the dirt color map is both tileable and seamless. So, once again, you need to perform the image tile test as you did for the sand color map earlier. You need to choose Select|All, choose Edit/Define Pattern, create a new file that's 600×600 pixels, and then fill the new image with the pattern. You can see the results in Figure 11.8.

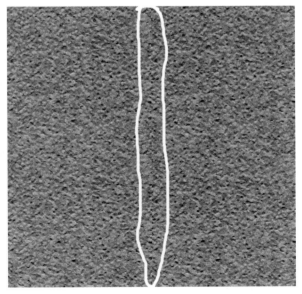

Figure 11.7 The Color layer after changing its Hue and Saturation (see figure in Color Studio).

Figure 11.8 The tile test for the dirt color map. The seam is circled (see figure in Color Studio).

You're not quite as fortunate here as you were with the sand color map. The circled area shows where a seam appears down the center of the image. To make the dirt color map seamless, you need to follow a few steps:

1. With the Rectangular Marquee tool, select the far left of the Color layer all the way from top to bottom and in about 59 pixels to the right, as shown in Figure 11.9.

2. Copy this portion, and paste it into a new layer.

3. Select Layer|Transform|Flip Horizontal.

4. Slide the flipped section all the way over to the right side. To constrain the layer's movement to only the vertical axis, use the right arrow key on your keyboard. (To make the portion move 10 pixels each time you press the arrow key, try holding down the Shift key simultaneously [Ctrl key for Windows].) Make sure that you slide this portion so that it meets up exactly with the far right side of your image—not one pixel short or one pixel too far. One way to be sure that you get the portion placed exactly on the far right side is to make the layer beneath it (the Color layer) invisible, and use the right and left arrow keys until you're sure the portion meets up exactly with the far right side, as shown in Figure 11.10.

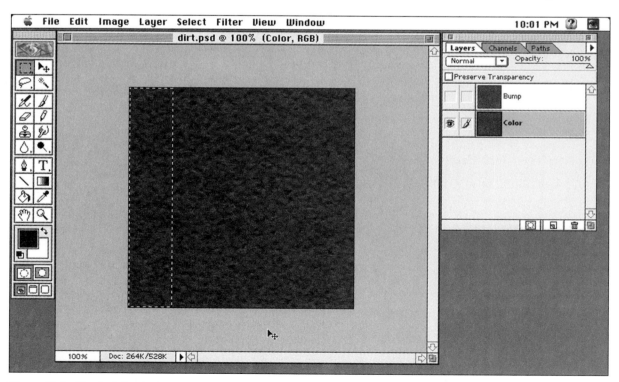

Figure 11.9 The far left selection.

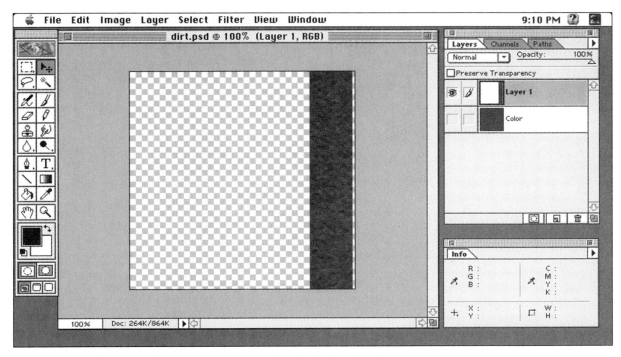

Figure 11.10 Making sure the portion meets up exactly with the far right side.

5. From the Layers palette, make the Color layer active, and then link the portion layer to the Color layer. Then, select the Merge Linked command from the Layers palette.

6. Perform the seamless tile test on the Color layer.

   You'll see that the image is now truly seamless. At this point, your color layer should resemble Figure 11.11.

Now you need to create the bump map for the dirt to simulate its texture in 3D.

Creating The Dirt Bump Map

Create the dirt bump map as follows:

1. Make sure that the Color layer is active. From the Layers palette, select Duplicate Layer to create an exact duplicate of the Color layer.

2. Name the duplicate layer "Bump".

3. Select Image|Adjust|Hue/Saturation. In the dialog box, turn down the Saturation all the way to -100 (leaving the other sliders alone).

4. Because the grays in the Bump layer are still too washed out for this example, select Image|Adjust|Brightness/Contrast. In the dialog box, crank up the Contrast to +27 (leaving the Brightness slider alone). At this point, the Bump layer for the dirt should look like Figure 11.12.

Figure 11.11 The completed Color layer for the dirt.

Figure 11.12 The completed Bump layer for the dirt.

That completes the work you need to do for both the color and bump maps of the dirt. Now, all you need to do is to save the layers in a format that your 3D program can read so that the image maps can be applied onto the 3D ground object that you've created. Once again, I simply planar-mapped the Color and Bump layers onto a flat, 3D plane.

Now that you've gotten your hands a little dirty with the dirt maps, you can move on to creating some rock and mineral maps.

Creating Rock And Mineral Texture Maps

Rocks are combinations of minerals that form solids with all kinds of different properties, depending on the minerals that they're made up of. Most geologists exclude soil, which comes from eroded and broken-down rocks, from the rock category.

Rocks are classified into three categories: Igneous, Sedimentary, or Metamorphic, according to how they were formed. Igneous rocks come from solidified molten magma or lava. When a volcano blows, it spews forth molten lava, which cools and we get igneous rock.

Sedimentary rock is formed when a bunch of sediment particles that have eroded from rocks (like sand) settle. Coal is a sedimentary rock that is formed from the remains of plants or animals.

Metamorphic rock is formed through heat, pressure, and/or chemical changes. They're a result of the folding of the earth's plates. When embarking on a texturing job, it helps to learn the origin and history of the textures you'll be creating. In this way, you'll have a much more thorough image in your mind's eye with which to work.

Finding Resource Material For Natural Textures

Although the Internet can be a great aid in finding resource materials for textures, using it can also be a big waste of time. For one thing, if you're lucky enough to find pictures of what you're looking for, the images are either GIFs or JPEGs, which are usually the lowest quality images you can find. Both GIF and JPEG images are made smaller by color reduction. Usually, for 3D texture mapping, you need 32-bit (millions of colors) images that have never been compressed. When I went searching for some resource imagery of rocks on the Internet, I searched for "rocks+pictures." What I got were 10,000 sites with pictures of various rock bands beginning with Hanoi Rocks. Frustrated, I took a nice stroll outside and easily found several great rocks to bring home as reference materials—free of charge and no copyright infringement. I dropped the rocks (carefully) onto my scanner's glass face to get the resource images shown in Figure 11.13.

Figure 11.13 The resource imagery of some found rocks.

All too often, people rely on technologies like the Internet when they could save themselves a lot of time by looking for resources in their own backyards. Looking for natural textures like leaves and rocks on the Internet or in books seems ludicrous when they are actually all around you just as soon as you step outside. With rock resources in hand, you can now create a seamless and tileable color map that can be used on just about any rock surface you create.

Creating The Rock Color Map

Because a rock is made up of a conglomeration of minerals, using the previously created dirt color map as a starting point makes sense. Here's how to get started:

1. Open the Dirt.psd file if it's not already open. You can delete the Bump layer.

2. Make the Color layer active by clicking on it in the Layers palette.

3. Select Filter|Noise|Dust & Scratches. Set a Radius of 14 pixels and a Threshold of 24 Levels. These settings should reduce some of the crevices in the rock's color.

4. Change the color for the rock so that it doesn't appear too similar to the dirt map—just in case you decide to put the two together in one scene. To do so, select Image|Adjust|Hue/Saturation. In the dialog box, change the Hue to -146, the Saturation to -39, and the Lightness to +11. These settings should give you a basic rock color (see Color Studio for example).

5. Select Filter|Sharpen|Sharpen More to enhance the grain of the rock.

6. Add some variation to the color by using Photoshop's painting tools. Create a subdued purple foreground color, RGB 87, 67, 87.

7. Double-click on the Airbrush tool, and give the airbrush the following settings:

- Change from Normal to Overlay

- Pressure: 4%

- Diameter: 35 pixels

- Hardness: 0%

- Spacing: 25%

- Default Angle and Roundness

8. Airbrush some of this color lightly over the rock pattern from left to right (see Color Studio for example).

9. Create a new bluish color, RGB 67, 84, 91, and apply the blue using the same Airbrush tool (see Color Studio for example).

10. Add some dark "pock" marks to the rock's surface. To do so, double-click on the Burn tool icon, and give it these settings:

- Midtones

- Exposure: 84%

- Diameter: 3 pixels

- Hardness: 100%

- Spacing: 25%

- Default Angle and Roundness

These marks should resemble the ones shown in Figure 11.14.

11. To create a little more chaos to the rock's texture, select Filter|Noise|Add Noise. Then, set the Amount to 14, select Gaussian, and check the Monochromatic box.

12. Add a few white marks to contrast the dark marks. Change the foreground color to white, and select a Paintbrush with the following settings:

- Normal

- Opacity: 80%

- Diameter: 3 pixels

Figure 11.14 Adding the dark "pock" marks to the rock with the Burn tool.

- Hardness: 100%

- Spacing: 4%

- Default Angle and Roundness

See the completed rock color map in the Color Studio for the results of how the image should look after applying the white.

13. Save the rock image as "Rock.psd".

You've now completed the painting portion of the Color layer of the rock, but you still need to make sure that this image is both tileable and seamless. After running the tile test (as you did for both the sand and dirt image maps), you'll notice that a seam appears between the top and bottom portions of the map. To fix it, simply copy the top portion of the image into a new layer, flip it vertically, move it to the bottom of the image, and blend it in with the Eraser tool as you did before. (See the Color layer in the Color Studio for the results of this operation.)

Now that you've completed the Color layer for the rock, you need to add some texture to the rock's surface.

Creating Rock Bump Maps

Even a rock that feels relatively smooth has some texture to it. That being the case, be sure to create a bump map for any rock surface that you create. Bump-mapped textures can save you a lot of time because creating a bump-mapped texture is usually much more intuitive than modeling textures. Because you've already created a good color map for the rock, use it as the basis of the bump map. Here's how to get started:

1. Open the Rock.psd file if it's not already open.

2. Make sure that the Color layer is active by clicking on it, and select Duplicate Layer from the Layers palette menu. Rename the new layer "Bump".

3. Select Image|Adjust|Hue/Saturation. In the dialog box, change the Saturation to -100.

4. Select Image|Adjust|Brightness/Contrast. In the dialog box, increase the Contrast to +24. Take a look at Figure 11.15 to see what the final bump map for the rock should look like.

Save both the Color and Bump layers as separate image files that your 3D program can read, and then cubic-map them onto your rock shape. To see the results of the rock textures mapped onto a simple rock shape, take a look at Figure 11.16.

Now, you've completed your work on the rock, so you can move on to creating another predominant part of nature's landscape, the leaf.

Creating Leaf Color Maps

As is true with so much of nature, the variety of leaves is nearly endless. There are dull leaves, shiny leaves, fat leaves, skinny leaves; they

Figure 11.15 The final bump map for the rock (see figure in Color Studio).

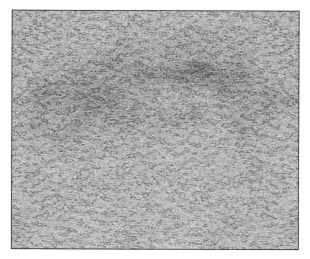

Figure 11.16 The color and bump maps for the rock cubic-mapped onto a simple 3D rock surface (see figure in Color Studio).

come in all shapes and sizes and nearly every hue on the color wheel. Just take a short walk outside, and explore the variety of leaf shapes, colors, and textures. For this tutorial, you'll re-create a fairly common leaf, ivy. Ivy has a fairly large, shiny leaf and can be found carpeting the ground or growing up the sides of buildings. Figure 11.17 shows a picture of a leaf of ivy for reference.

1. Create a new file, and name it "Leaf.psd".

2. Create a new layer, and name it "Color".

3. Delete the Background layer so that just the Color layer is present.

4. Choose Select|All, and fill the layer with a green color, RGB 19, 43, 0.

5. To define the shape of the leaf, open the file called Leafshape.psd, which you can find in chapt11\Leaf on the companion CD. After you open this file, choose Select|All; then, copy and paste it as a new layer into your Leaf.psd file. Use this file along with Figure 11.17 to help guide the painting process.

6. As you can see in the ivy image in Figure 11.17 , you need to re-create all the veins in the leaf by hand. To do so, create a new light green color, RGB 72, 100, 15, for the veins.

7. Create a new Paintbrush with the following settings:

   • Normal

   • Opacity: 100%

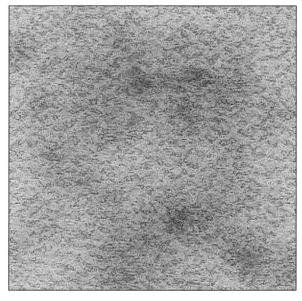

Figure 11.17 A leaf of ivy.

- Diameter: 3 pixels
- Hardness: 100%
- Spacing: 4%
- Default Angle and Roundness

8. Make the Color layer semitransparent by changing its Opacity to 90%. The black-and-white image of the leaf now should be visible through the Color layer, as shown in Figure 11.18.

9. With the new Paintbrush, paint some veins emanating from the base of the leaf out toward the far edges of the leaf. After you lay down the major veins, change the brush settings as follows:

- Normal
- Opacity: 68%
- Diameter: 1 pixel
- Hardness: 100%
- Spacing: 10%
- Default Angle and Roundness

10. If some of your lines didn't terminate as well as you might have liked, use the Smudge tool with the following settings to terminate the lines:

Figure 11.18 Looking through the Color layer to use the black-and-white leaf image as a guide (see figure in Color Studio).

- Normal

- Pressure: 68%

- Diameter: 9 pixels

- Hardness: 0%

- Spacing: 8%

- Default Angle and Roundness

At this point, the Color layer for the leaf should look like Figure 11.19.

11. To add a little chaos to the color of the leaf, select Photoshop's Burn tool, and give it the following settings:

- Midtones

- Exposure: 26%

- Diameter: 27 pixels

- Hardness: 0%

- Spacing: 25%

- Default Angle and Roundness

With the Burn tool, follow the veins of the leaf so that the Color layer resembles Figure 11.20.

Figure 11.19 The Color layer for the leaf after painting the veins.

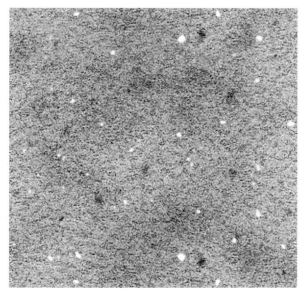

Figure 11.20 The Color layer for the leaf after applying the Burn tool (see figure in Color Studio).

Note: *If your 3D program does not support clip maps, use the black-and-white silhouette as a transparency map.*

12. Apply some noise to the leaf's color to further enhance the chaotic distribution of the color. Select Filter|Noise|Add Noise. Then, set the Amount to 5, select Gaussian, and check the Monochromatic checkbox.

You've now completed your work on the leaf's Color layer. See Figure 11.21 to get an idea of what the finished color map for the leaf should look like.

13. Be sure to set the Opacity of the Color layer back to 100% before saving it. After you save the Leaf.psd file, you're ready to move on to creating the bump map for the leaf.

Creating The Leaf Bump Map

You can create the leaf bump map as follows:

1. From the Layers palette, select Duplicate Layer to get an exact copy of the leaf's color.

2. Rename this layer "Bump".

3. Select Image|Adjust|Hue/Saturation. In the dialog box, drag the Saturation slider all the way to the left (-100). This setting removes all the color from the Bump layer.

4. Select Image|Adjust|Invert to invert the values in the Bump layer. Inverting gives you a somewhat ghostly, pale image, as shown in Figure 11.22.

Figure 11.21 The final Color layer for the leaf (see figure in Color Studio).

Figure 11.22 The Bump layer after inverting it.

5. To fix the pale look of the Bump layer, select Image|Adjust|
   Brightness/Contrast. In the dialog box, decrease the Brightness
   to -100, and increase the Contrast to +43.

Now that you've finished the color and bump maps for the leaf, save
the Leaf.psd file. Also, save the black-and-white image that you added
as a guide layer. You will use this black-and-white silhouette of the leaf
as a clip map for the leaf shape.

Planar-map the color, bump, and clip maps onto a simple 3D plane.
To see what this image looks like, take a look at Figure 11.23.

Figure 11.23 The rendered image of the leaf (see figure in Color Studio).

Moving On

Of course, I simply do not have the space to cover a myriad of other
elements that occur in nature. Keep in mind that the trick to creating
realistic, natural image maps is in seeing. While you're out walking
around, try to perceive the world around you in terms of re-creating it
in the 3D realm. It can be both challenging and fun, and it's better
than walking around worrying about your last phone bill. In the next
chapter, you'll learn how to transform the geometry of your 3D object
by using displacement maps.

PART IV

SPECIALTY
TEXTURES

PAINTING
DISPLACEMENT
MAP TEXTURES

12

There's a little-known and rarely used feature in most midrange 3D programs that combines modeling with texture mapping. This is known as displacement mapping. With the use of a displacement map, you can actually alter the geometry of your 3D surface by creating a grayscale image.

In this chapter, I'll discuss several displacement mapping issues and techniques, including the following:

• Reviewing displacement maps

• Creating displacement maps for modeling

• Painting terrain

• Generating animated displacement maps

Overview Of Displacement Maps

Displacement maps are similar to bump maps in that a grayscale image is used to alter the surface elevation of a 3D object. The major difference between the two is that with a bump map, the surface elevation changes are more or less an illusion. Bump maps use the grayscale image to alter the surface normals of a 3D object to make the surface appear bumpy. If you use a bump map on a flat, 3D plane and look at it from the side, the plane will still appear to be flat, even though the 3D plane may look bumpy from a front view. In contrast, a *displacement map* actually distorts the physical, 3D geometry of an object. For the displacement map to distort the image, it requires a good deal of geometry with which to work. You can't have a 3D plane that's made up of a single patch or polygon and expect a displacement map to distort its surface.

Figure 12.1 shows a 3D plane consisting of 8,192 polygons. You'll use this 3D surface to planar-map the displacement image shown in Figure 12.2. When the displacement map is applied to the 3D plane, you get a result like that shown in Figure 12.3. If you flip the plane on its side, as shown in Figure 12.4, you see that it truly is no longer just a flat plane.

Notice that even at a polygon count of 8,192, the 3D plane still shows some of its polygon edges in the shadow areas. The number-one drawback in using displacement maps to deform a surface is that they require an extraordinary number of polygons or patches to work properly. As you know, increased polygon counts result in increased rendering times.

On the other hand, displacement maps can save you a great deal of time when you're modeling.

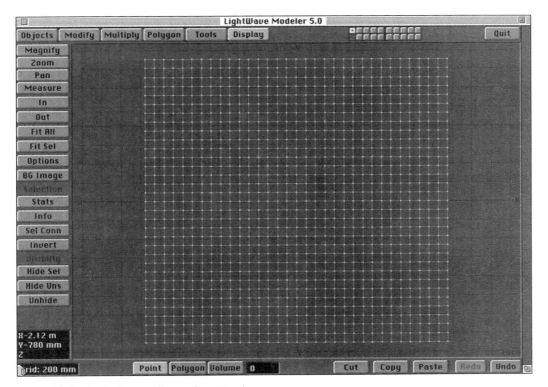

Figure 12.1 A 3D plane made up of 8,192 polygons.

Figure 12.2 The displacement map image.

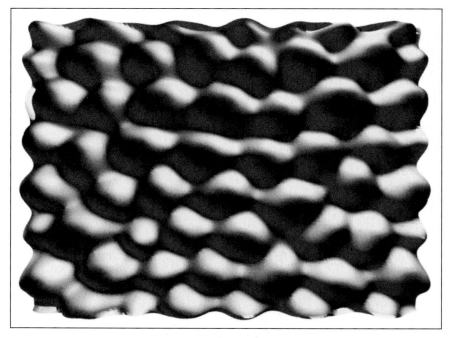

Figure 12.3 The displacement map applied to the 3D plane.

Figure 12.4 The 3D plane flipped on its side.

Creating Displacement Maps For Modeling

I think that most 3D artists would agree that painting a face is much easier than modeling one. Take a look at Figure 12.5.

Here, you see a grayscale image of a face that was painted in Photoshop for use as a displacement map. Something you should watch out for is the tendency to paint shadows on the character's face. As with a bump map, dark areas result in lower elevation, and light areas result in higher elevation. If you were to paint in the shadows, the character's face would have deep caverns in it wherever the shadows occurred. When you're painting displacement maps, try to think only in terms of elevation. Look at Figure 12.6 to see what the displacement map face looks like when it's applied to a flat, 3D plane made up of 32,768 polygons.

As you can see, this 3D face looks pretty good, even though no color, bump, specularity, or diffusion maps have been created for it.

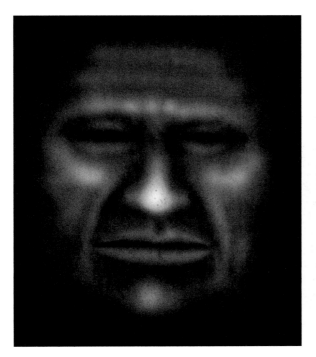

Figure 12.5 The displacement map for a 3D face.

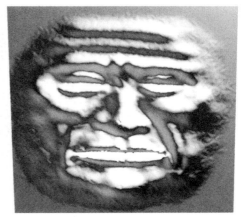

Figure 12.6 The results of using the displacement map (shown in Figure 12.5) applied to a 3D plane.

Displacement maps can be fantastic time-savers if used in the right situations. According to a source at Industrial Light and Magic (George Lucas' special-effects studio in San Rafael, California), in the *Mars Attacks* film, the visible brains of the 3D Martian creatures were created using displacement maps. The use of displacement maps makes a lot of sense in this instance if you consider the time it would take to model all the convolutions in a brain. In the popular game Myst, created by Cyan, all the terrain of the Myst island was created by using a single displacement map—which is understandable unless you need to physically model each and every rock crevice for the terrain. Displacement maps are most commonly used in this type of situation—to generate terrain. Moving on, you can explore the terrain displacement map further.

Painting Terrain

Generating photorealistic terrain displacement maps is actually quite simple with Photoshop. The following short tutorial will help you to get the hang of creating realistic terrain using displacement maps:

Note: *In general, if you're working with a 3D program on the
Mac, the program can import PICT
files—unless you're using
Lightwave, which can import only
TIFF files (unless you use a plug-in).
If you're working with a 3D program on the PC (Windows 95/
98/NT), in general the program
will be able to read Targa or TIFF
files. If you have not yet purchased
a 3D program, save your image
maps as Photoshop files and you'll
be able to convert them into a file
format the 3D program can read.*

1. To begin, create a new Photoshop file with a white background that is 600×600 pixels.

2. Press the D key on your keyboard to set the default colors: black in the foreground and white in the background.

3. Select Filter|Render|Clouds.

4. Click on the foreground color swatch, and change the color to a dark green, RGB 0, 122, 5.

5. Select Filter|Render|Difference Clouds. At this point, the image should look like Figure 12.7.

6. To remove all the color from the image, select Mode|Grayscale. The results of this operation should match Figure 12.8.

7. Create a 3D plane that consists of at least 20,000 polygons, as shown in Figure 12.9.

8. Save the grayscale displacement map for the terrain in a file format that your 3D program can use.

9. Planar-map the displacement map onto the 3D plane. Depending on the texture amplitude that you apply to the displacement map (I used .5 in Lightwave), your plane should look something like Figure 12.10.

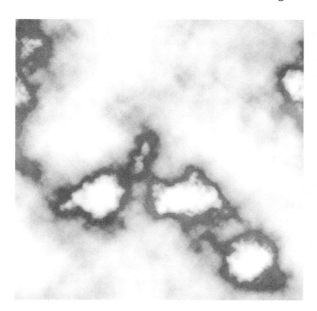

Figure 12.7 The terrain image after applying the Difference Clouds filter (see figure in Color Studio).

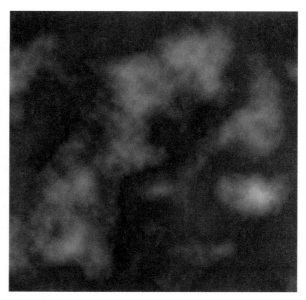

Figure 12.8 The terrain diffusion map after removing its color (see figure in Color Studio).

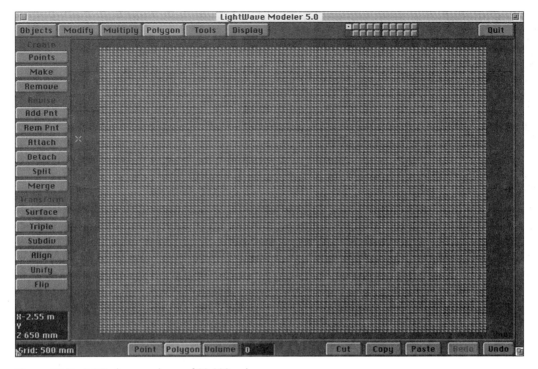

Figure 12.9   A 3D plane made up of 20,000 polygons.

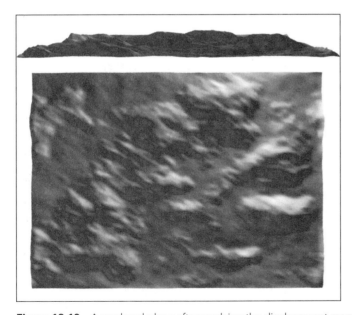

Figure 12.10   A rendered plane after applying the displacement map.

The terrain represented in Figure 12.10 may not look like a place you'd want to move to, but by changing the color of the 3D plane, the camera angle, and maybe adding a little fog, you should get a rendered terrain image resembling that shown in Figure 12.11.

Displacement maps are great for generating realistic terrain, but they can also be used in animating surfaces.

Generating Animated Displacement Maps

In this section, you'll explore a simple way that you can use a displacement map to generate a cool animation effect. Open the QuickTime movie called Facedisp.mov in the chapt12 folder on the companion CD-ROM. (If you do not have QuickTime, you can download it free from **www.quicktime.apple.com**.) In this short animation, you'll see a face that appears to emerge from a wall. To create this same effect, follow these few steps:

1. Open the file called Face.psd, and save it in a file format that your 3D program can read. As you can see, it is the same face image that you worked with at the beginning of this chapter.

2. Create a flat 3D plane made up of at least 30,000 polygons. These polygons create the wall from which the face will emerge.

Figure 12.11   The final rendered images of the terrain (see figure in Color Studio).

3. Build the ceiling, other walls, and any furniture you might want to add to the 3D scene.

4. Planar-map the diffusion map of the face onto the 3D plane (the one that's made up of 30,000 polygons).

5. Begin the animation with the displacement map's texture amplitude set to 0 at frame 0. The first frame rendered should look something like Figure 12.12.

6. Set the texture amplitude for the last frame of the animation (frame 120) so that the face has emerged from the wall, as shown in Figure 12.13.

   After you render all the frames of the animation, you should have a result matching that of the Facedisp.mov.

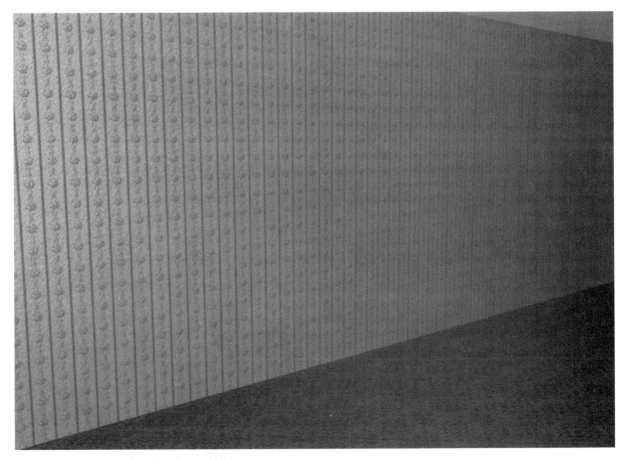

Figure 12.12   The rendered first frame of the animation.

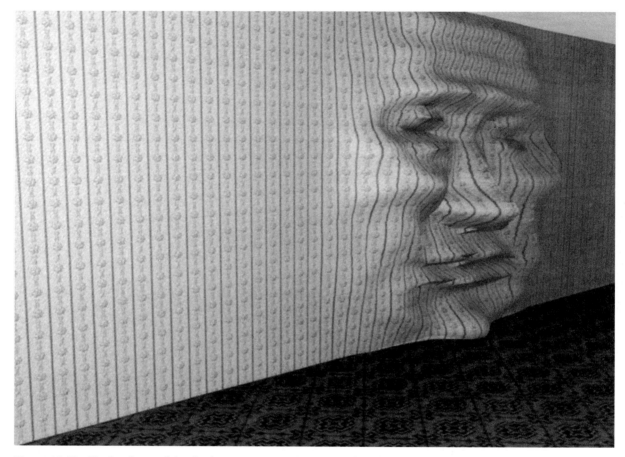

Figure 12.13 The last frame of the displacement map animation (see figure in Color Studio).

Moving On

In most cases, using a bump map is sufficient in creating the illusion that your 3D surface is physically distorted; however, when you need to modify the actual 3D surface, and modeling that surface would be either too time consuming or difficult, using the displacement map is the ideal solution. In the next chapter, you'll learn about light gels, which are another little-known but very useful way to achieve some fantastic 3D effects without costing you an arm and a leg in extra time and money on plug-ins for your 3D package.

PAINTING
LIGHT GELS
13

A good rule of thumb when you are creating 3D artwork and animation is: If it's not going to be seen by the camera, don't waste your time making it look perfect. There are, of course, many exceptions to this rule, but for the most part, you should not spend valuable time creating artwork that the viewer will never see.

Consider if you were composing a realistic forest scene, and you wanted to create the effect of sunlight passing through the leaves of the trees. You wouldn't want to model and surface every tree and leaf that the sunlight would hit just to create the shadows because those particular leaves and trees are behind the camera. How can you avoid the extra modeling and still achieve the shadow effect as if the sun were passing through the trees? Light gels to the rescue. *Light gels* allow you to use an image map to project the light through—much like projecting the light of a slide projector through a slide.

In this chapter you'll learn about the following light gel topics:

- Light gel basics

- Light shadow maps

- Images projected with light gels

- Light gel animations

Light Gel Basics

Light gels, also called *gobos*, have been used for years in the film industry. Remember the dramatic lighting in those film noir detective pictures in which the shadows from the venetian blinds created a series of angles behind the detective's desk? In most cases, these high contrast shadows were created using gels something like those shown in Figure 13.1 to project light to create the shadows.

As you've probably noticed, lights in the 3D world don't behave exactly like the lights in the real world, so to achieve a better shadow effect for the light gel, I've added some Gaussian Blur with a Radius of 2.6 to create the light gel shown in Figure 13.2.

Light Shadow Maps

Light gels are great tool for creating complex shadows for a scene—not to mention all the time you'll save because you don't have to model all the shadow-casting objects. To better understand how light gels work, you should create one. One of the most useful light gels is the leaf shadow light gel mentioned previously.

Creating A Leaf Shadow Light Gel

Follow these steps to get started:

1. Create a new Photoshop file with a white background that's 800×800 pixels square. You need to make your shadow map images at least this large so that when the image is projected, the

Figure 13.1 The light gel for a film noir scene.

Figure 13.2 The film noir light gel with Gaussian Blur applied.

pixels in the image become evident because the light gel will be stretched over the 3D surfaces that it is projected onto. The light gel's stretching depends on how far away the light is from the 3D surfaces that the light hits.

2. Press the D key on your keyboard to set the default colors (black in the foreground and white in the background).

3. Select Filter|Render Clouds. The image should now look like Figure 13.3.

4. Select Filter|Artistic|Paint Daubs. Set the Brush Size to 5, Sharpness to 34, and the Brush Type to Sparkle. The image should look like Figure 13.4 at this point.

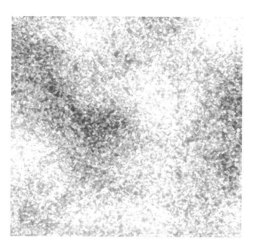

Figure 13.3 The image after applying the Render Clouds filter (see figure in Color Studio).

Figure 13.4 The image after applying the Paint Daubs filter (see figure in Color Studio).

5. Because the image is still a little too washed out, select Image| Adjust|Brightness/Contrast. In the dialog box, set the Contrast to +31, and leave the Brightness at 0.

6. Because the dark areas of the image will create shadows, you need to soften their edges. To do so, select Filter|Blur|Blur More. The results should match Figure 13.5 at this point.

7. If you've never worked with light gels in your 3D program, be sure to check the program's manual to see how different types of lights allow you to load light gels into them. Also, be sure to check out how the light projects the light gel by doing several test renders. Some 3D programs allow you to load a light gel only into a spot-light. As the light gel that you just created exists now, it may render

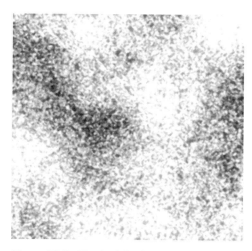

Figure 13.5 The leaf shadow light gel (see figure in Color Studio).

by cutting off the perimeter edges of the image quite sharply; this effect belies the realism of the outer edge shadow. To fix this problem, press the D key to set the foreground color to black.

8. Double-click on the Airbrush tool to open its palette, and apply the following settings:

   - Normal

   - Opacity: 50%

   - Diameter: 65 pixels

   - Hardness: 0%

   - Spacing: 25%

   - Default Angle and Roundness

9. Use the Airbrush to darken the outer edge of the image, as shown in Figure 13.6.

Figure 13.6 The final leaf shadow light gel (see figure in Color Studio).

You've now completed the work on the leaf shadow light gel. Save the file in a format that your 3D program can read; then load the image as a light gel into one of your lights that supports light gels.

I've created a simple scene consisting of a flat 3D plane and a cow to demonstrate how the leaf light gel affects the objects within the scene. First, take a look at what the rendered scene looks like without the light gel in Figure 13.7.

Of course, the scene would greatly benefit from the addition of some actual 3D trees. To help illustrate the shadows that are created by this particular light gel, I've omitted them. Figure 13.8 shows the scene rendered with the leaf shadow light gel applied to a spotlight.

As you can see, the leaf shadows that are cast by the light gel you just created can greatly enhance the realism of an outdoor scene without bogging down your machine with increased rendering time.

Another way to enhance your scenes with light gels is by using them to influence the color of the scene. To do so, you can load a color image into a light source and then project it onto a scene.

Figure 13.7 The rendered scene without the leaf shadow light gel (see figure in Color Studio).

Figure 13.8 The rendered scene with the light gel applied to a spotlight (see figure in Color Studio).

Projecting Images With Light Gels

What might be a good situation or scene in which you would want to use an image that is projected by a light? Perhaps you want to create a psychedelic effects scene in which the light appears as a swirling kaleidoscope of color. This scene is sort of a throwback to the sixties, but just use it as an example.

First, you need to create the light gel that you can project onto the scene.

Creating A Psychedelic Projected Image Light Gel

1. Create a new Photoshop file that is 800×800 pixels. Make sure that the background is set to white.

2. Click on the foreground color, and change it to a bright red, RGB 255, 0, 0.

3. Select Filter|Texture|Stained Glass. Use the following Options settings:

   - Cell size: 24

   - Border Thickness: 14

   - Light Intensity: 3

   The results should match Figure 13.9.

4. Double-click on the Magic Wand Tool. Set the Tolerance to 32, and make sure that the Anti-alias button is checked.

5. With the Magic Wand Tool, click on the white area of one of the cells, as shown in Figure 13.10.

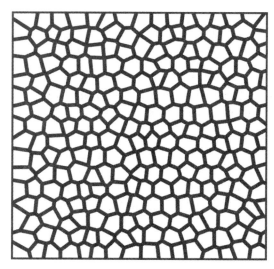

Figure 13.9 The light gel after applying the Stained Glass filter (see figure in Color Studio).

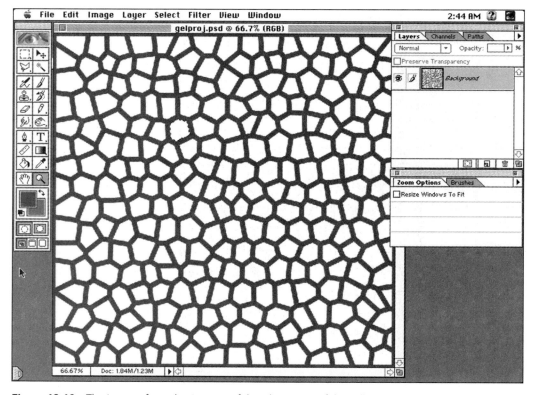

Figure 13.10 The image after selecting one of the white areas of the cell.

6. Choose Select|Similar so that the rest of the white areas become selected, as shown in Figure 13.11.

7. Click on the foreground color, and change it to a light blue, RGB 0, 198, 255.

8. Choose Edit|Fill, Set Contents to Use Foreground Color, set Opacity to 100%, and set the Mode to Normal (see the Color Studio for what the image should look like after you've added light blue color).

9. The image is a little rough on the eyes at this point. But, it's supposed to be psychedelic. Select Filter|Distort|Twirl, and set the Angle to 394 degrees. The image should look something like Figure 13.12 at this point.

10. Click on the foreground color, and change it to a light purple, 255, 0, 240.

11. Select Filter|Render|Difference Clouds. The image should look like Figure 13.13 at this stage.

12. Because the image has some jagged edges on the swirl, you should fix them by choosing Filter|Blur|Gaussian Blur. Apply a Radius of 1.6 pixels.

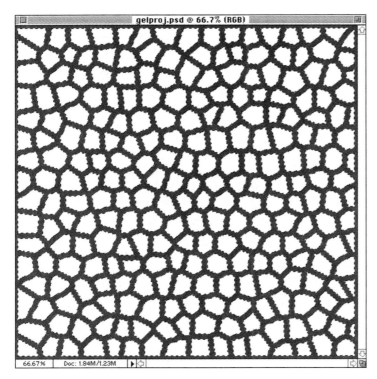

Figure 13.11 The image after selecting the Similar command.

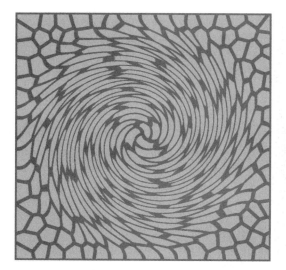

Figure 13.12 The image after applying the Twirl filter (see figure in Color Studio).

Figure 13.13 The image after applying the Difference Clouds filter (see figure in Color Studio).

You've completed the work to create your psychedelic light gel. Now, it's time to see the light gel in action. You need to save the image in a format that your 3D program can read and then attach the image to the main light in the scene. I threw together a little scene made up mainly of boxes and cylinders to illustrate the effect that the light gel will have. Figure 13.14 shows the scene rendered without the light gel.

Figure 13.15 shows the same scene with the psychedelic light gel applied. The coolest thing that you can do with light gels is to use them to create animated effects.

Light Gel Animations

You can animate light gels in two ways. You can either physically animate the light that's projecting the gel, or you can animate the gel. By rotating the light, you can achieve a kaleidoscopic effect throughout the scene. The other method is to animate the light gel as a series of frames that are loaded into the light as a sequence of gels.

Figure 13.14   The scene without the psychedelic light gel.

Figure 13.15   The scene with the psychedelic light gel.

Moving On

Light gels are not the most common of all the image mapping methods. If you experiment with them, though, you'll find that in many situations light gels can save you many hours of modeling and image mapping time.

This being the final chapter of the book, I hope that the new image mapping techniques and Photoshop knowledge that you've acquired will help you to tackle even the most ambitious 3D texturing jobs with a new-found confidence, zeal, and creativity. I'm also hoping that this book will soon become dog-eared through extensive use and reference. There are many more topics, techniques, and an endless variety of procedures that can be used to get the results that you want, but this book should supply you with a comprehensive primer of some of the best ways to enhance the realism of your 3D artwork and animation with the use of texture maps and Photoshop. The following appendix contains listings of where you can find Web sites, plug-ins, and books that can help you to extend your knowledge of 3D image mapping procedures and the power of your 3D program.

APPENDIX:
GRAPHICS
RESOURCES

The following books, magazines, and Web sites may be useful to you as a 3D artist.

Books

Character Animation In Depth

Doug Kelly
Softcover, $59.99
The Coriolis Group, 1998
ISBN: 1566047714

3D Creature Workshop

Bill Fleming
Softcover, $49.95
Charles River Media, 1998
ISBN: 1886801789

The Illusion Of Life

Frank Thomas and Ollie Johnston
Revised
Hardcover, $60.00
Hyperion, 1995
ISBN: 0786860707

Animation: From Script To Screen

Shamus Culhane
Reprint Edition
Paperback, $14.95
St. Martin's Press, 1990
ISBN: 0312050526

The Human Figure In Motion

Eadweard Muybridge
Hardcover, $24.95
Dover Publications, 1989
ISBN: 0486202046

Drawing On The Right Side Of The Brain: A Course In Enhancing Creativity And Artistic Confidence

Betty Edwards
Paperback Revised Edition, $15.95
J. P. Tarcher, 1989
ISBN: 0874775132

Experimental Animation: Origins Of A New Art

Robert Russet and Cecile Starr

Reprint Edition

Hardcover, $14.95

Da Capo Press, 1988

ISBN: 0306803143

Animals In Motion

Eadweard Muybridge

Hardcover, $29.95

Dover Publications, 1957

ISBN: 0486202038

Magazines

3D Artist

www.3dartist.com

3D Design Magazine

www.3d-design.com

Animation World Network

www.awn.com

Computer Graphics World

www.cgw.com

Digital Magic

www.cgw.com/cgw/Archives/Magic/1998/06/06toc1.asp

Visual Magic

visualmagic.awn.com

Textures

Here are some great sources of textures that you can find on the Internet:

avalon.viewpoint.com/

axem2.simplenet.com/

texlib.povray.org/

www.visi.com/~drozone/jewel2.html

3D Software Programs

Alias|Wavefront's Animator, PowerAnimator, Designer, AutoStudio, Studio, StudioPaint, Eclipse and Sketch

www.aw.sgi.com/pages/home/index.html

Avid Technology's Softimage

www.softimage.com

Martin Hash's Animation Master

www.hash.com

NewTek's LightWave 3D

www.newtek.com

My Email

eyemhear@pce.net

INDEX

D

E

F

G

H

PHOTOSHOP 5
3D TEXTURES
F/X AND DESIGN

COLOPHON

From start to finish, The Coriolis Group designed *Photoshop 5 3D Textures f/x and design* with the creative professional in mind.

The cover was created on a Power Macintosh using QuarkXPress 3.3, Adobe Photoshop 5, Alien Skin Black Box 2 filters, and the Trajan and Futura font families. It was printed using four-color process, metallic silver ink and spot UV coating.

The interior layout was also produced on a Power Macintosh with Adobe PageMaker 6.52, Microsoft Word 98, Adobe Photoshop 4, and Adobe Illustrator 7.0.1. The body text is Stone Informal, heads are Avenir Black, and chapter titles are Copperplate 31ab.

Photoshop 5 3D Textures f/x and design was printed by Courier Kendallville, Inc. of Kendallville, Ind.

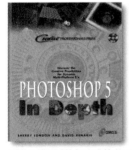
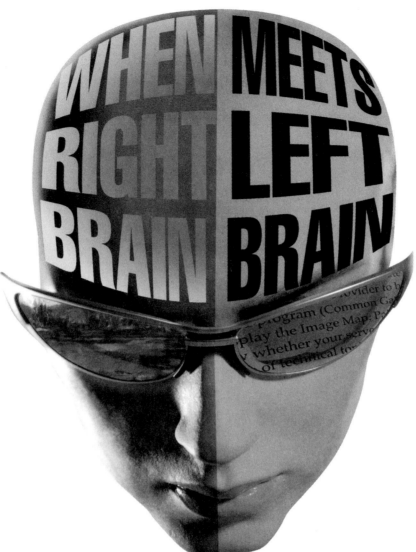

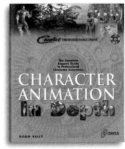

What's On The CD-ROM

The companion CD-ROM for *Photoshop 5 3D Textures f/x and design* contains:

- ▶ Super realistic 3D models of human faces ready for texture mapping.

- ▶ 3D models (in a variety of 3D formats) of creature accessories ready for texture mapping.

- ▶ Drop-your-jaw creature models in a variety of 3D formats ready for texture mapping.

- ▶ Dozens of wireframe templates (in Photoshop format) to help you get started with the image mapping process.

- ▶ A multitude of seamless and tileable texture maps for you to use in your 3D creations.

- ▶ Trial editions of Adobe Photoshop 5, Adobe Illustator, and Adobe After Effects

System Requirements

PC:

Hardware:
- ▶ 486 or better preferred
- ▶ Windows 95/98 or later; or Windows NT 4.0 or later
- ▶ 32MB of RAM

Software:
- ▶ Adobe Photoshop 5.0
- ▶ 3D software of your choice

(Individual applications may have different requirements.)

Macintosh:

Hardware:
- ▶ PowerPC preferred
- ▶ MacOS 7.5 or later
- ▶ 32MB of RAM

Software:
- ▶ Adobe Photoshop 5.0
- ▶ 3D software of your choice

(Individual applications may have different requirements.)

See the *readme* files on the CD for acknowledgments, descriptions, installation instructions, and other important information.

For future updates to the CD contents, go to **www.coriolis.com/errata** and enter the ISBN 1576102742.